STAR QUILTS
Outside the box

HEXAGON PATTERNS FROM THE KANSAS CITY STAR

by Edie McGinnis

STAR QUILTS, VOLUME 3   KANSAS CITY STAR BOOKS

Star Quilts: Outside the box

Hexagon Patterns from The Kansas City Star
Star Quilts, Volume 3

By Edie McGinnis

Photography by Tammy Ljungblad

Book Design by Jeff Dodge

Edited by Doug Worgul

Published by KANSAS CITY STAR BOOKS
1729 Grand Boulevard
Kansas City, Missouri, USA 64108

First edition

Library of Congress Card Number: 2001088516

ISBN 0-9709131-0-9

Printed in the United States of America
by Walsworth Publishing Co.

To order copies, call StarInfo. (816) 234-4636

www.kcstar.com

www.pickledish.com

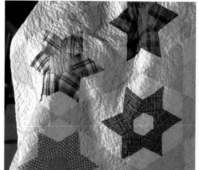 

On the cover: Boutonniere. Owned by Warren Cromer, Overland Park, Kansas. Title page: Boutonniere. Owned by Marilyn Zerwekh, Lawrence, Kansas.

table *of* contents

Oklahoma Star.
Owned by Reylene Harbit,
Warrensburg, Missouri.

introduction

From the late 1920s and into the 1960s *The Kansas City Star* published hundreds of quilt patterns that have become the basis of treasured family heirlooms and have perpetuated a cherished cultural tradition.

Kansas City Star patterns have been indexed and reprinted over the years in various forms by various groups. In 1999, *The Kansas City Star* decided to publish its own book on these renowned patterns. *Star Quilts* told the history of the patterns and presented redrafts so modern-day quilters could make their own Stars and more. It was a smash hit.

Yet there were too many Stars — more than 1,000 were printed in the newspaper through the years — and too much history for a single book. Too much for two books for that matter. *Star Quilts* II was published in 2000, and still we haven't come close to exhausting the supply of our great patterns.

In these pages you'll find a selection of new redrafts and cutting instructions, all easy to understand and colorfully illustrated, for 20 quilts that weren't in the first two books. But these patterns are just a bit different, as our author and expert quilter Edie McGinnis explains.

not your ordinary sampler

Every quilt show I hear about I try to visit. I love looking at the work of other quilters. Sometimes it's so extraordinary and marvelous I feel incompetent and envious. Then there will be the amazingly ugly quilt that leaves me wondering what in the world was the quilter thinking.

One thing I've noticed is that among all the quilts hanging in all the shows I've attended there's always at least one sampler quilt, and usually more. The samplers are typically made of different blocks, some with sashing, some without. Some will be made of scraps; some will have all the colors coordinated.

They all have one thing in common. The blocks are all square. Perhaps it's time to "think outside the box." Every once in awhile its fun to stretch our capabilities and challenge ourselves

by trying something different in a sampler. In my research of *The Kansas City Star* quilt patterns I found many blocks that didn't fit the classic square classification. I've chosen 20 of these patterns that form hexagons and have redrafted them to a nine-inch block. Each pattern will fit with the others to make a hexagonal sampler quilt or make a lovely quilt by itself by repeating the same block.

Some of these blocks are quite easy and some are fairly difficult, but they're not labeled as such because I don't want to discourage anyone from the adventure of trying a particular pattern. There are times when we find ourselves amazed at what we can do when we just jump into it with both feet. Have a great time quilting "outside the box." - *Edie McGinnis*

Right, face page: Boutonniere doll quilt. Owned by Judy Streu, Liberty, Missouri.

patterns
and templates

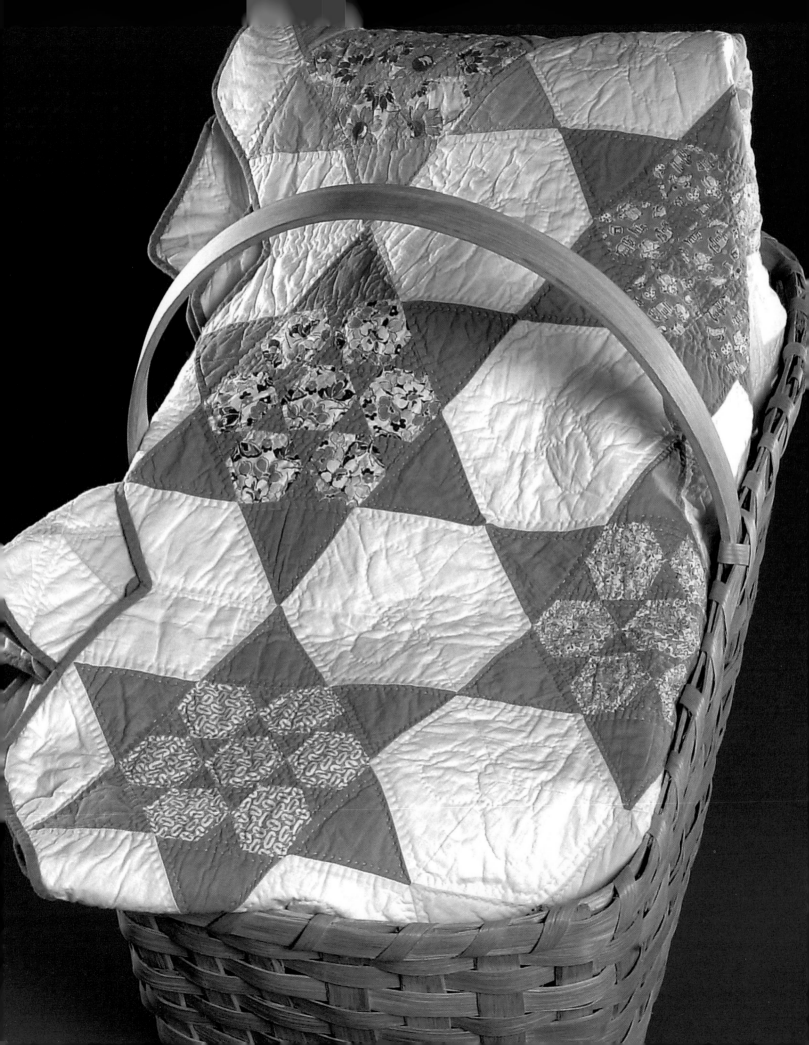

the 1936 hidden star

"My love affair with quilts started when I was in my thirties, about the time of the American quilt revival. My first remembrance of them was when I went away to college; my loving grandmother offered me a few quilts to take with me. I graciously took them, but I didn't love them like I do now. As a collector, I adore their history and charm. I wish now that I had asked my grandmother more about our family quilts and the quilters who made them." -*Judy Streu,* Liberty, Missouri.

Left, face page:
Hidden Star.
Owned by Judy Streu,
Liberty, Missouri.

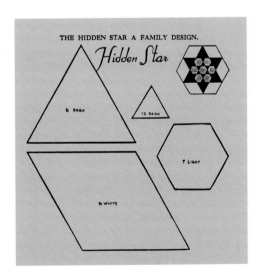

Published July 4, 1936

July 4, 1936, *in The Star...*President Franklin Roosevelt gave a speech at Monticello marking the 110th anniversary of Thomas Jefferson's death and the 160th anniversary of the nation's birth. ● A plate glass window at the Downtown theater in Kansas City was broken by melons and tomatoes thrown by some rowdies. ● Two local boys were held for disturbing the peace by exploding firecrackers at an Independence Day celebration.

cutting and piecing
the 1936 hidden star

Block size
9 inches

Fabrics needed
light, medium and dark

Cut
from light fabric, cut six diamonds using **template B**.

Cut
from medium fabric, cut seven hexagons using **template A**.

Cut
from dark fabric, cut six large triangles using **template C** and twelve small triangles using **template D**.

Note
It is recommended that all seam lines be marked for accuracy.

1. In the center of the block there are three rows of hexagons and triangles. For the top row, sew two (D) triangles to an (A) hexagon as shown. Then sew two (D) triangles to an (A) hexagon as shown. Sew these two units together to comprise row one.

2. Sew row two together by adding (D) triangles to (A) hexagons as shown.

3. Sew row three together by adding (D) triangles to (A) hexagons as shown.

4. Sew the three rows together to complete the center of the block.

5. Sew the large (C) triangles to the hexagon as shown.

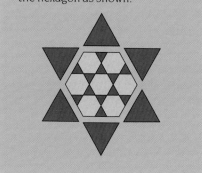

6. Inset the large (B) diamonds to finish the block.

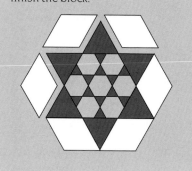

Quilter's wisdom
"Always sign your quilt; it is a work of art." - *Sara Gibb*

quilting templates for
the 1936 hidden star

Arrow Heads block. Made by Edie McGinnis, Kansas City, Missouri.

the 1942 arrow heads

Published January 21, 1942

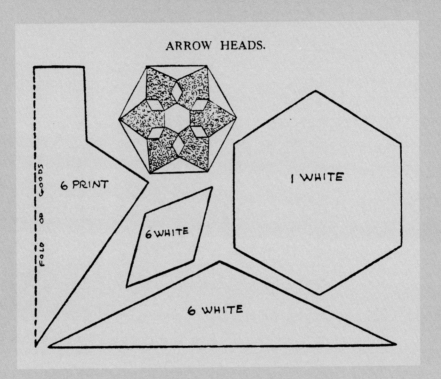

"The effectiveness of 'Arrow Heads' is best sustained by choosing prints with very small figures rather than those with large designs." -*The Kansas City Star*

January 21, 1942, in The Star...The United States Commerce department revealed a massive hemisphere-wide war plan including trade, currency and production strategies. ● Allied warships shelled Japanese forces as they invaded Malaysia. ● Funeral services were held for actress Carole Lombard and her mother killed in an airplane crash in Nevada.

cutting and piecing
the 1942 arrow heads

Block size
9 inches

Fabrics needed
light, medium and dark.

Cut
from light fabric cut center hexagon
using **template A** and six diamonds
using **template B**.

Cut
from medium fabric, cut six triangles
using **template C**.

Cut
from dark fabric, cut six arrowheads
using **template D**.

Note
It is recommended that all seam
lines be marked for accuracy.

1. Clip the seam of the arrowhead
about three times, once before the
corner, once at the corner, and
once after the corner. This will
make pivoting the diamond easier
and help the block lie flat.

2. To the right side of each arrowhead, sew a light (B) diamond and
make six units that look like this.

3. Sew each of the arrowhead units
to the center hexagon.

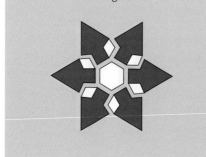

4. Sew the side seams around the
diamonds. Inset the (C) triangles
to finish the block.

5. The final hexagon block.

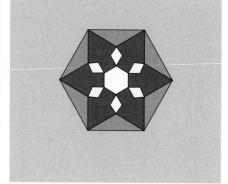

Quilter's wisdom
"When pinning seams together
so they meet and butt perfectly,
pin a 32nd of an inch away from
the seam so the points will
match." -*Joyce Holley*

quilting templates for
the 1942 arrow heads

A

B

C

D

the 1938 old-fashioned wheel

Left, face page:
Old-Fashioned Wheel.
Owned by Butterfield
Youth Services,
Marshall, Missouri.

"Many talented hands have made this a true friendship quilt to benefit the children of Butterfield Youth Services in Marshall, Missouri. Betty Lenz, an internationally known quilter, donated the antique blocks. The quilt was designed by the Country Patchwork Quilt Guild in Marshall, Missouri, and hand quilted by Naomi Sims of Odessa, Missouri.

"Our quilt project was started in 1987 with the donation of a sampler quilt made by Margaret Nelson of Kingsville, Missouri. In 1990 we started sending a quilt block pattern in our July newsletter. The first year we received 250 blocks. Last year we received 2,000 blocks. Friends and quilt clubs take the blocks and design quilt tops. Others hand or machine quilt them.

"The finished quilts are then sold at our annual Quilt Auction, Barbecue and Duck Race in Marshall, Missouri. It is our only fundraiser.

"Quilts are given to the children and they all say, 'I can't believe anyone cares enough about me to make me a quilt.' " *-Butterfield Youth Services*

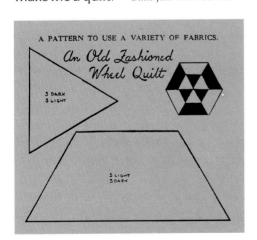

Published January 8, 1938
*That day in The Star...*2,000 rebel soldiers and their families surrendered to Spanish government troops after a 17 day siege at Teruel, Spain. ● Union workers vandalized produce trucks in a labor dispute in Kansas City's city market. ● The Chrysler, Ford, and Hudson automobile companies announced that they would call back some of the workers laid off before the Christmas holidays.

the 1938 old-fashioned wheel

Block size
9 inches

Fabrics needed
light, a dark or a print.

Cut
from light fabric, cut three parallelograms using **template B** and three triangles using **template A**.

Cut
from dark or print fabric cut three parallelograms using **template B** and three triangles using **template A**.

Note
It is recommended that all seam lines be marked for accuracy.

Quilter's wisdom
"Thread your entire package of needles on your spool of thread. Fasten in the little notch. Pull off the 18" length you need for sewing. Put the empty needles in the pin cushion and when all the needles are used, start over."
-*Donna Scranton*

1. Sew a light (A) triangle to a dark or print (B) parallelogram. Make three units like this. We'll call this **A Unit**.

2. Sew a dark or print (A) triangle to a light (B) parallelogram. Make three units like this. This will be **B Unit**.

3. Sew A and B **Units** together alternating units. Three units will make one half of the block. Sew the two halves together to complete the hexagon.

4. The final hexagon.

quilting templates for
the 1938 old-fashioned wheel

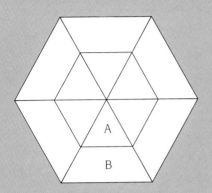

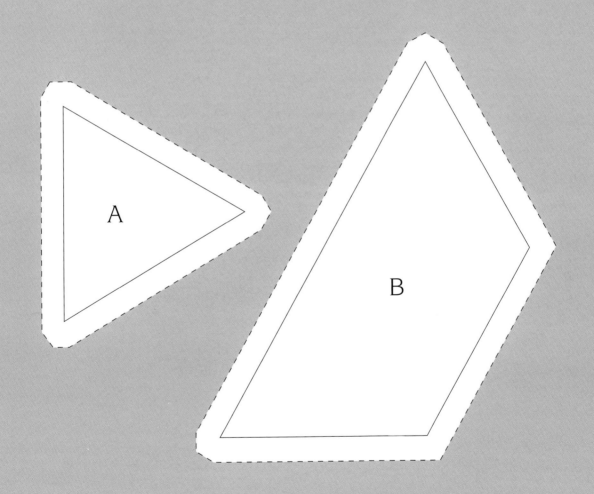

Six-Pointed Star block. Made by Grace Spencer, Lexington, Missouri.

the 1938 six-pointed star

Published October 5, 1938

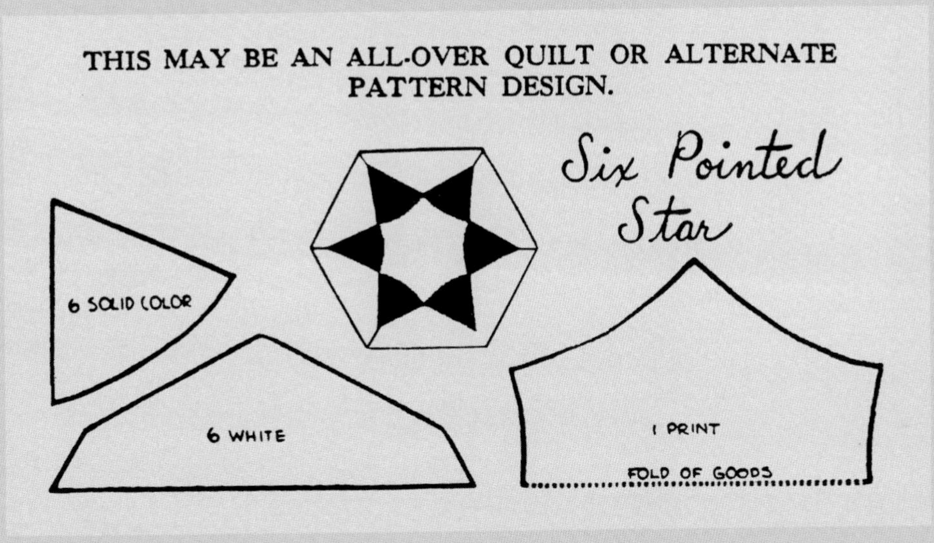

THIS MAY BE AN ALL-OVER QUILT OR ALTERNATE PATTERN DESIGN.

6 SOLID COLOR

6 WHITE

Six Pointed Star

1 PRINT

FOLD OF GOODS

"This pattern makes for an attractive all-over quilt. Use the 'Six-Pointed Star' pattern in three colors, or set it together with strips of material. Be sure to allow room for seams."
-The Kansas City Star

*October 5, 1938, in The Star...*Hitler continued pursuit of his fraudulent territorial claims against Czechoslovakia. ● Reflecting naive optimism for world peace, investors sparked a gain on New York stock markets of $1 to $2 a share. ● The New York Yankees won the first game of the World Series against the Chicago Cubs, 3-1.

the 1938 six-pointed star

Block size
9 inches

Fabrics needed
light, medium, and dark.

Cut
from light fabric cut center piece
using **template B**.

Cut
from medium fabric, cut six flower
petals using **template A**.

Cut
from dark fabric, cut six triangles
using **template C**.

Note
It is recommended that all seam
lines be marked for accuracy.

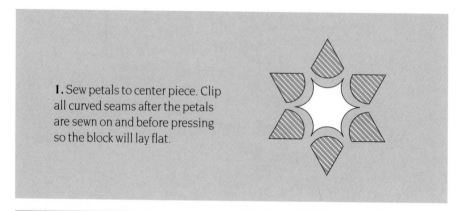

1. Sew petals to center piece. Clip
all curved seams after the petals
are sewn on and before pressing
so the block will lay flat.

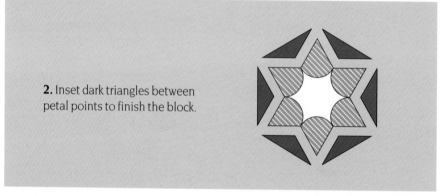

2. Inset dark triangles between
petal points to finish the block.

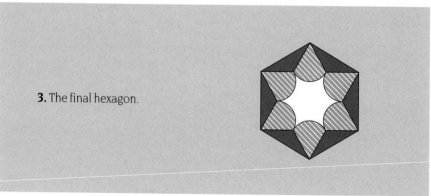

3. The final hexagon.

Quilter's wisdom

"To make perfect, uniform knots in your thread, make 3-6 wraps of the thread tail around your threaded needle. Grip
the wrapped thread tightly between the finger and thumb and slide it out to the end of the thread. Voila!"
-*Rosemary Garten*

quilting templates for
the 1938 six-pointed star

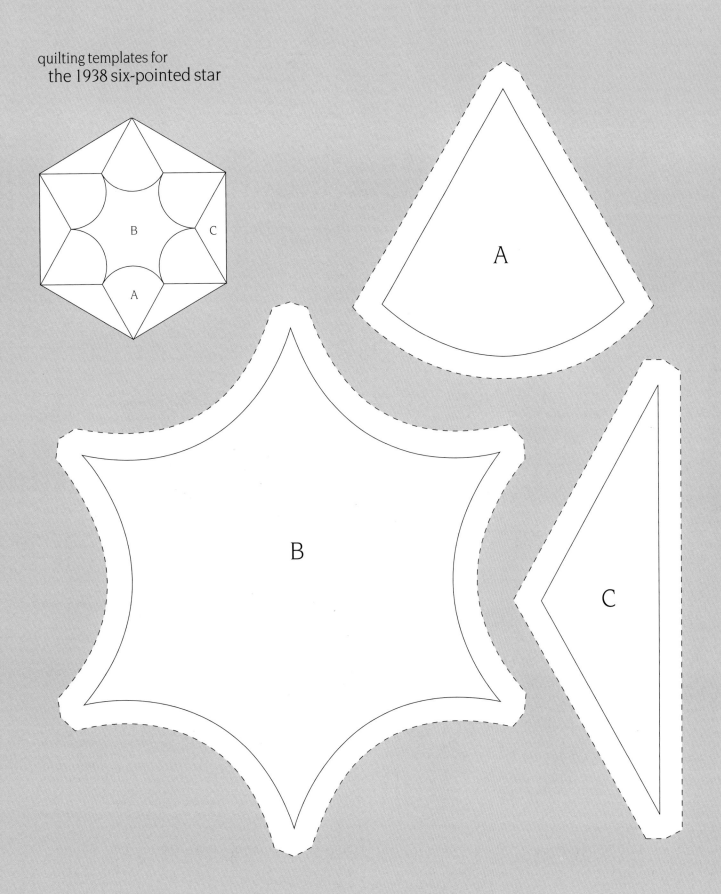

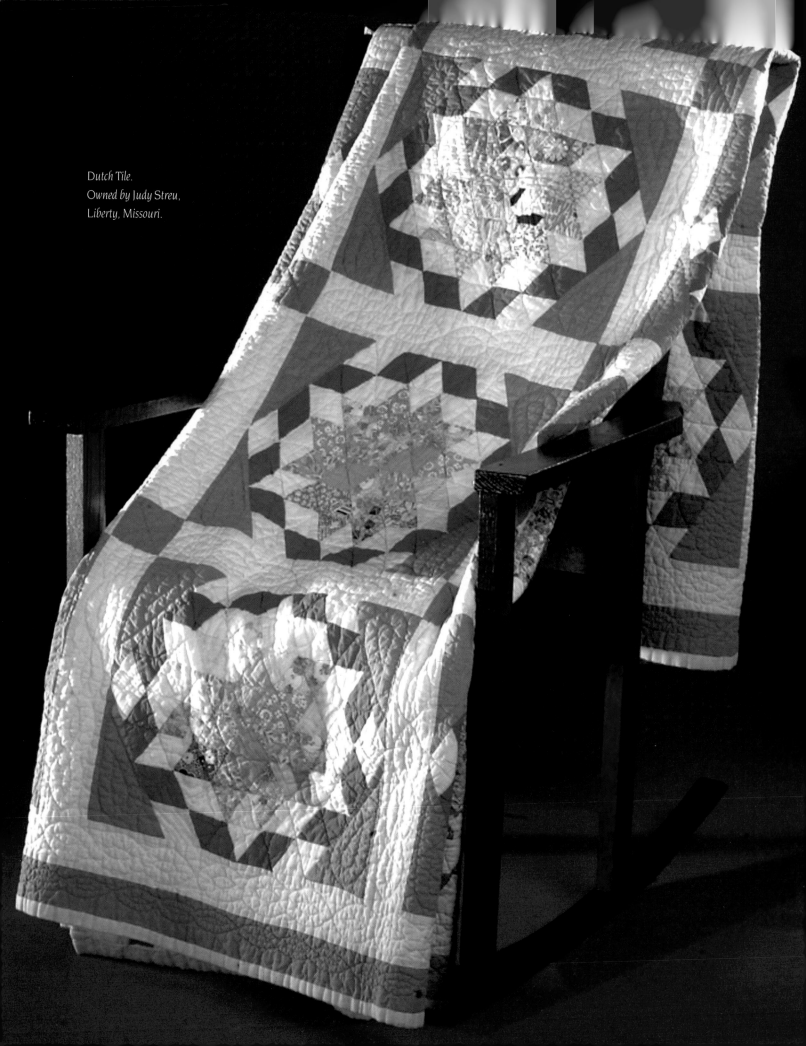

Dutch Tile.
Owned by Judy Streu,
Liberty, Missouri.

the 1931 dutch tile

"A simple block affords many diversions. Many pretty tile patterns can be made using this simple patch and combining various colors and fabric. The two shown below suggest the interesting possibilities that it affords. The block measures sixteen inches across and is set together with equilateral triangles, which fit the side of the hexagon. Allow for seams." *-The Kansas City Star*

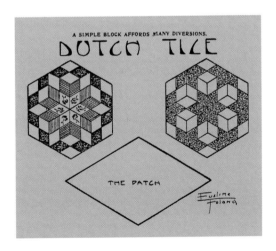

Published October 31, 1931

*That day in The Star...*Oil prices were hiked 15 cents bringing the cost to 85 cents a barrel. ● Fourteen nations, including the United States, agreed to a world disarmament truce sponsored by the United Nations. ● Federal narcotics agents seized a shipment of apples after discovering tubes of drugs hidden in them.

cutting and piecing
the 1931 dutch tile

Block size
9 inches

Fabrics needed
light, medium and dark.

Cut
from light fabric, cut 18 diamonds using **template A.**

Cut
from medium fabric, cut 24 diamonds using **template A.**

Cut
from the dark fabric, cut six triangles with **template C.**

This block will be divided into two units, A and B. Make six **A Units** and six **B Units.**

Note
It is recommended that all seam lines be marked for accuracy.

Quilter's wisdom
"When threading a sewing machine needle moisten your finger and hold it opposite the thread and it will pull the thread through the needle."
-*Millie Hohimer*

1. A Unit: Sew one light diamond and one medium diamond together. Then sew one medium diamond to one light diamond. Sew the two pieces together to make the unit.

2. B Unit: Sew one medium diamond to one light diamond. Sew one dark diamond to one medium diamond. Sew the four diamonds together to make one large diamond.

3. Sew three **B Units** together to form one half of the center star.

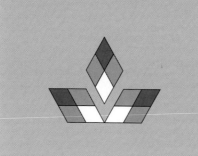

4. Sew three **B Units** together to form the other half of the star. Sew the two halves together.

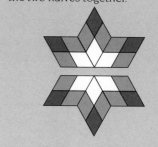

5. Inset the **A Units** between the points of the star as shown.

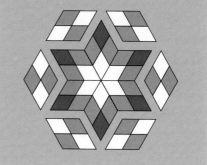

6. The final hexagon block.

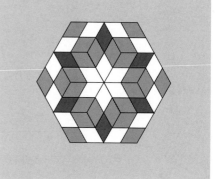

quilting templates for
the 1931 dutch tile

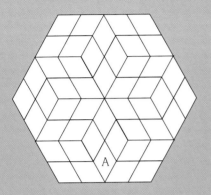

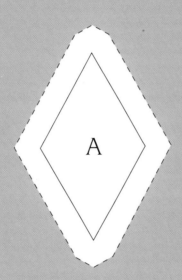

Glory Block. Made by Sue McNamara, Peoria, Illinois.

the 1933 glory block

Published September 30, 1933

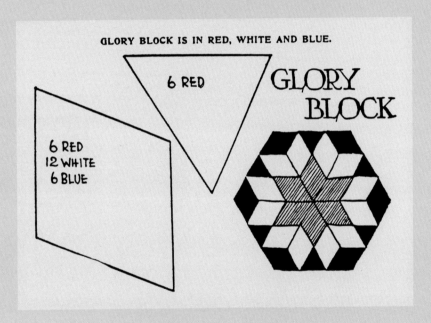

"The center is a blue star, all pieces are triangles and diamonds. Allow for seams."
-The Kansas City Star

September 30, 1933, in The Star..."Stratostat," a Russian balloon returned, from a world record flight of 11.8 miles above Earth. ● Missouri State Senator M. E. Casey announced his opposition to a state tax increase. ● Dr. Jabez Jackson denied the Pla-Mor ballroom's request for an "iceathon" in which men and women in bathing suits would compete against one another to see who could sit on a block ice longest.

cutting and piecing
the 1933 glory block

Block size
9 inches

Fabrics needed
light, medium and dark.

Cut
from light fabric, cut twelve diamonds using **template A** and six triangles using **template B**.

Cut
from medium fabric, cut six diamonds using **template A**.

Cut
from dark fabric, cut six diamonds using **template A**.

Note
It is recommended that all seam lines be marked for accuracy.

Quilter's wisdom
"To make corners that meet, always make a dot at the seam line and stick a pin straight through the dots on each patch. Only remove the pin when you stick the needle in the same hole." -*Ruby Downing*

1. Make six **A Unit**s by sewing three diamonds, a light, a medium and a dark together as shown and set aside.

2. Sew three light diamonds together to make first half of center star.

3. Sew three more light diamonds together to make the second half of the center star. Sew the two halves of the star together.

4. Inset an A Unit section between each of the star points.

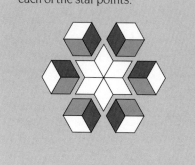

5. Inset light (B) triangles between each of the **A units**.

6. The final hexagon block.

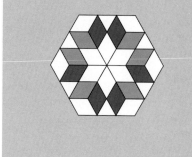

quilting templates for
the 1933 glory block

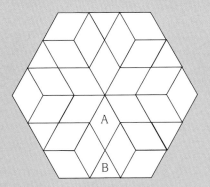

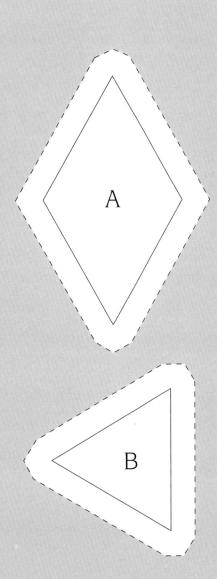

A

B

Whirligig.
Owned by Judy Streu,
Liberty, Missouri.

the 1936 whirligig

Published September 9, 1936
(Also known as the 1943 Texas Trellis)

That day in The Star... Kansas governor and Republican presidential nominee, Alf Landon, who celebrated his 49th birthday on this day, launched an aggressive attack on Franklin Roosevelt's "New Deal." ● Kansas City political boss Tom Pendergast underwent a second operation for relief of an intestinal obstruction. ● Ten Palestinians and three British policemen were killed in gun battles in Northern Palestine.

cutting and piecing
the 1936 whirligig

Block size
9 inches

Fabrics needed
light, a dark or a print.

Cut
from light fabric, cut six triangles using **template A.**

Cut
from dark fabric or prints, cut six parallelograms using **template B.**

Note
It is recommended that all seam lines be marked for accuracy.

1. Sew one (A) triangle to one (B) parallelogram. Make six of these units.

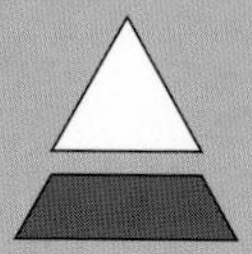

2. Sew three units together to make the first half of the block then sew the other three units together to make the other half of the block. Sew the two halves together to complete the block.

3. The final hexagon.

Quilter's wisdom

"For an accurate 1/4" seam, use 1/4" masking tape. Put the machine needle down and lay a strip of 1/4" tape to the right of the needle. Lay a second strip of tape to the right of the first strip. Remove the first strip and place it on top of the second strip. This makes a double layer of tape and creates a seam guide to run your pieces against."
-*Ruth Lofgren*

quilting templates for
the 1936 whirligig

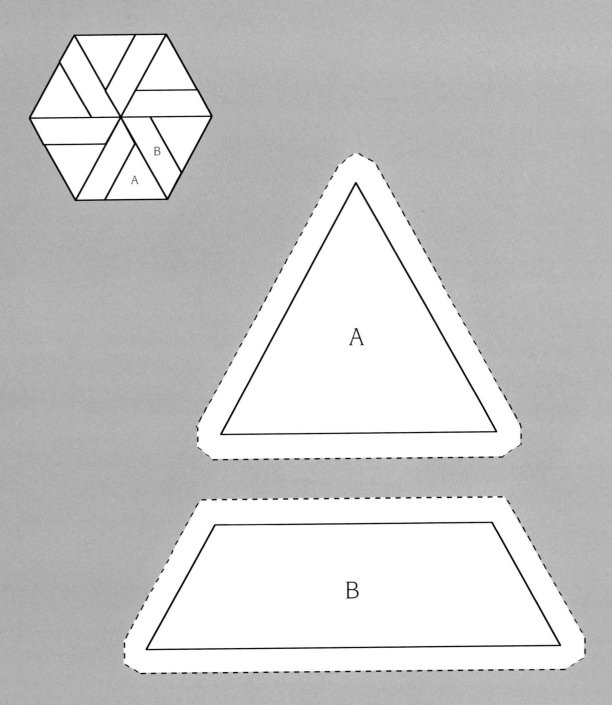

Morning Star. Made by Peggy and Corky Hutinett, Raytown, Missouri.

the 1936 morning star

Published February 1, 1936

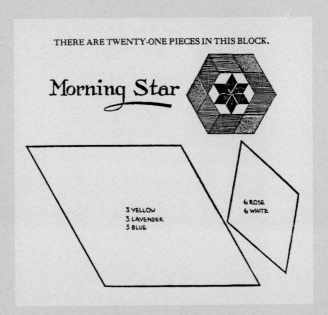

" 'Morning Star' is a pattern contributed by Mrs. Claude Davis, Moore, OK. This quilt sometimes is made in a color scheme of white, lemon, banana and dull orange but Mrs. Davis suggests you use the hues of early spring flowers, the crocuses, violets, daffodils and snowdrops that spring up with the morning star on warm, rainy mornings." *-The Kansas City Star*

*February 1, 1936, in The Star...*Former Brig Gen. William "Billy" Mitchell died of a heart attack while crossing the street in New York City. ● "Rose Marie," the movie starring Jeanette MacDonald and Nelson Eddy, was released. In it, they sang their most famous duet, "The Indian Love Call." ● 1,500 people were stranded on ice-bound Tangier Island in frozen Chesapeake Bay

the 1936 morning star

Block size
9 inches

Fabrics needed
light, medium, assorted prints and dark.

Cut
from light fabric, cut three diamonds using **template B** and six small diamonds using **template A**.

Cut
from medium fabric, cut three diamonds using **template B**.

Cut
from dark fabric, cut three diamonds using **template B**.

Cut
from assorted prints, cut six diamonds using **template A**.

Note
It is recommended that all seam lines be marked for accuracy.

Quilter's wisdom
"When quilting on your machine, wear surgical gloves to guide the piece through the machine. This will give you full control over your project. Your fingers will not slip and you can still pick up pins, etc." -*Peggy Huttinet*.

1. Sew three print diamonds together to form first half of inside star.

2. Sew the other three print diamonds together to form the other half of the inside star. Sew the two halves of the star together.

3. Inset small light diamonds between the star points as shown.

4. Sew a large light diamond to a large dark diamond. Make three units like this.

5. Sew a medium diamond to the center hexagon. Then sew a two-diamond unit to the center hexagon. Add another medium diamond and another two-diamond unit. Finish the block by adding the last medium diamond and two-diamond unit.

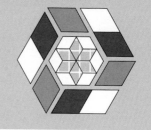

6. The final hexagon block.

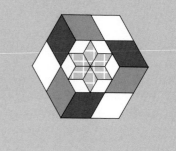

quilting templates for
the 1936 morning star

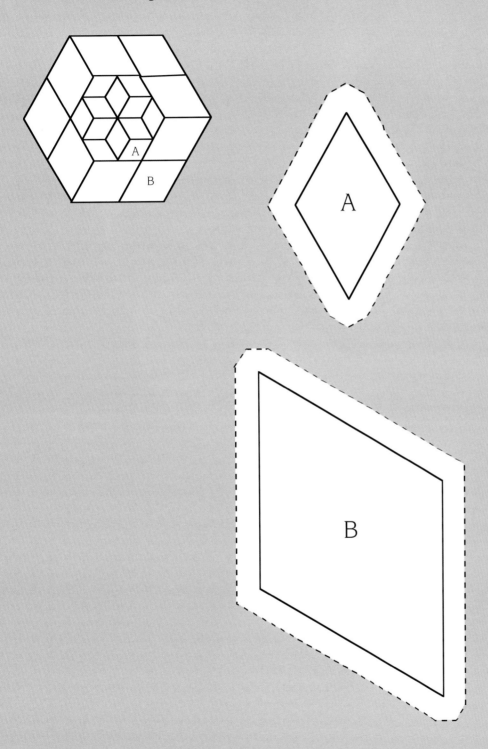

the 1930 spider web

"I purchased this quilt at an auction/fund raiser for the Salvation Army Children's Shelter located at 101 Linwood. This is an example of the type of quilt the volunteer quilters make for each child that enters the shelter - to keep forever. Each quilt has a small heart appliqued on it showing the love given to each child by the whole group of individuals it takes to assemble each quilt." -*Susan Benson, Overland Park, Kansas*

Spider Web.
Made by volunteer quilters
at the law firm of Shook,
Hardy and Bacon.

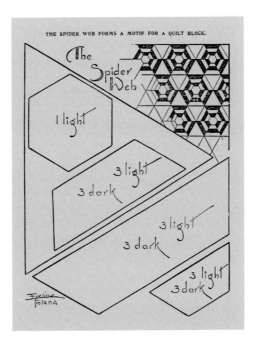

Published October 11, 1930

*That day in The Star...*A Kansas City grand jury investigated local charges of voter fraud. ● Pilots J. Errol Boyd and Harry Connor landed their plane, the Columbia, in London, only the second time a monoplane had successfully crossed the Atlantic. ● A Kansas City streetcar careened down Rockhill Road and smashed into a Nash sedan critically injuring a 19 year old man.

the 1930 spider web

Block size
9 inches

Fabrics needed
light and a dark.

Cut
from light fabric cut three parallelograms using **template B**, three parallelograms using **template C**, three parallelograms using **template D** and one hexagon using **template A**.

Cut
from dark fabric cut three parallelograms using **template B**, three parallelograms using **template C**, and three parallelograms using **template D**.

Note
It is recommended that all seam lines be marked for accuracy.

1. We will be making two units, A and B. To make **A Unit**, sew a light parallelogram (D) to a dark parallelogram (C). Add a light parallelogram (B). This unit will look like this: Make three of these units.

2. To make **B Unit**, sew a dark parallelogram (D) to a light parallelogram (C). Add a dark parallelogram (B). This unit will look like this: Make three of these units.

3. Sew the units to the hexagon alternating **A Unit** and **B Unit** leaving the side seams open. When all units are sewn to the center hexagon, sew the side seams to finish the block.

4. The final hexagon.

Quilter's wisdom
"Use the correct needle for the project you are working on. If you're quilting use "betweens." If you are appliquéing, use an applique needle, etc."
-*Anonymous*

quilting templates for
the 1930 spider web

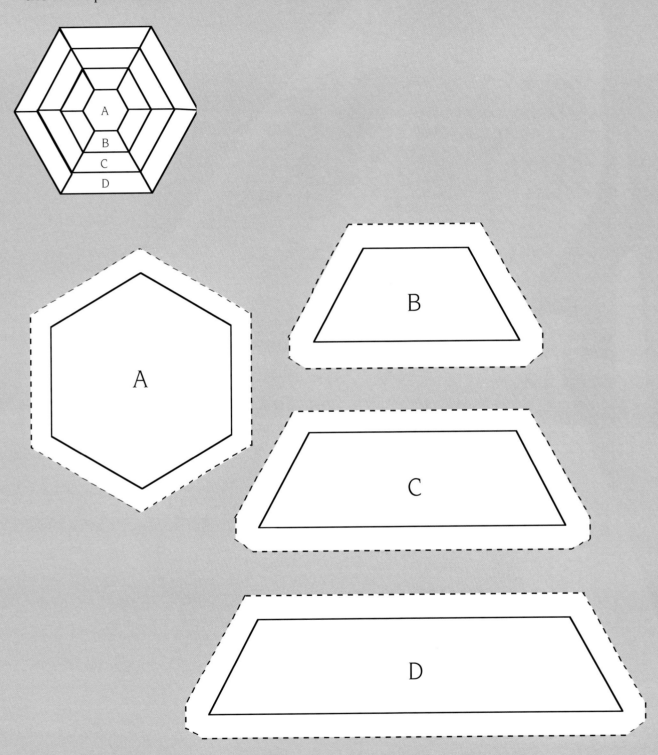

Whirligig.
Made from vintage feed
sacks by Edie McGinnis.

the quilter's gallery

The back of Edie McGinnis' feed sack Whirligig.

Top left, clockwise: Old-Fashioned Wagon Wheel block, made by Donna Walz, Kansas City, Missouri; Boutonniere block, made by Clara Diaz, Independence, Missouri; Spider Web block, made by Arlene Johnson, Kansas City, Missouri; Whirligig block, made by Mary Ellen Bloomquist, Independence, Missouri.

Left, facing page. Boutonniere doll quilt. Owned by Judy Streu, Liberty, Missouri.

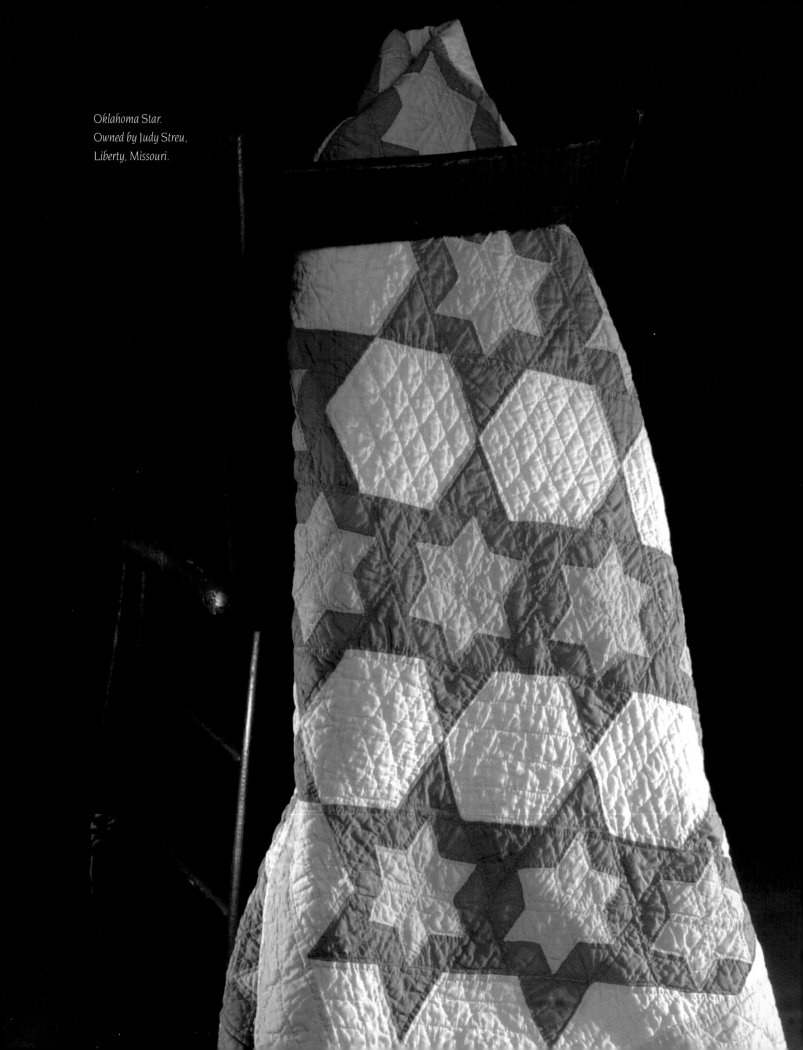

Oklahoma Star.
Owned by Judy Streu,
Liberty, Missouri.

Boutonnieres. Owned by Rosemary Warren Cromer, Overland Park, Kansas.

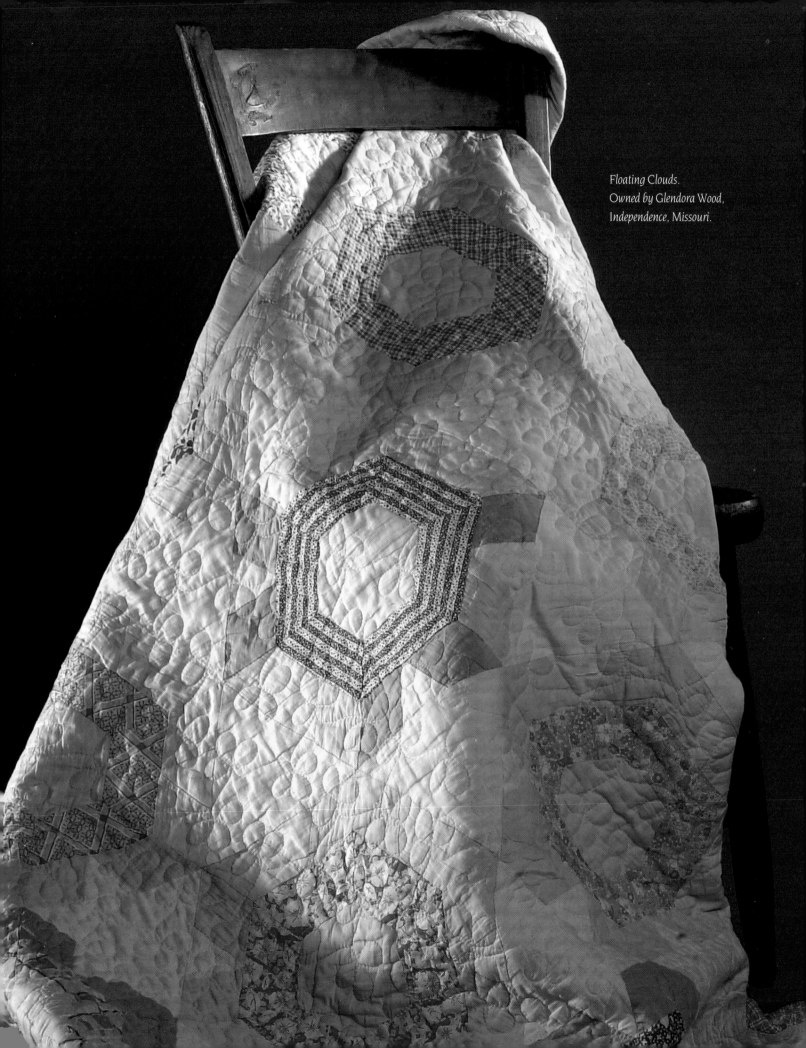

Floating Clouds.
Owned by Glendora Wood,
Independence, Missouri.

the 1938 floating clouds

"This quilt was pieced by my grandmother. She devised a quilt pattern from a small design on a handkerchief. She sent the pattern to *The Kansas City Star Weekly Farmer*. The pattern was chosen to be published in 1938. Gram lived with my family many years and she was special to me. At the time she sent in the pattern, we lived in Eldon, Missouri." *-Glendora J. Wood, Independence, Missouri*

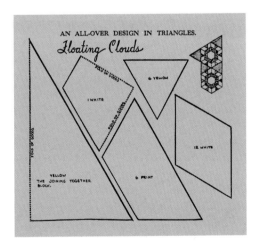

Published November 23, 1938

*That day in The Star...*Adolf Hitler signed yet another pact promising no further land claims on French territory. ● In the Spanish Civil War, eight rebel warplanes bombed Barcelona, killing 31 people. ● The Vatican sent an envoy to London to enlist British support in the church's conflict with Germany regarding mistreatment of German Catholics.

cutting and piecing
the 1938 floating clouds

Block size
9 inches

Fabrics needed
light, medium and dark.

Cut
from light fabric, cut one hexagon using **template** A and six triangles using **template** B.

Cut
from medium light fabric cut six parallelograms using **template** C. Make sure your fabric is layered rather than folded. If it is folded when you cut it, half of your pieces will be reversed and won't work. From medium fabric cut six parallelograms using **template CR**. Again, make sure your fabric is layered rather than folded.

Cut
from dark fabric, cut six parallelograms using **template D**.

Note
It is recommended that all seam lines be marked for accuracy.

Quilter's wisdom
"Measure twice and cut once. This works just as well for quilters as it does for carpenters." -*David Dutz*.

1. Sew strip (CR) to triangle (B). Add strip (C) to the opposing side of the triangle.

2. Sew strip (D) to the top of the triangle you have just made. Make a total of six units like this.

3. Sew the units to the center triangle leaving the side seams open until all units are sewn on. Then sew the side seams to complete the block.

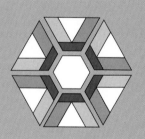

4. The final hexagon.

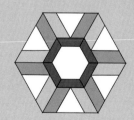

quilting templates for
the 1938 floating clouds

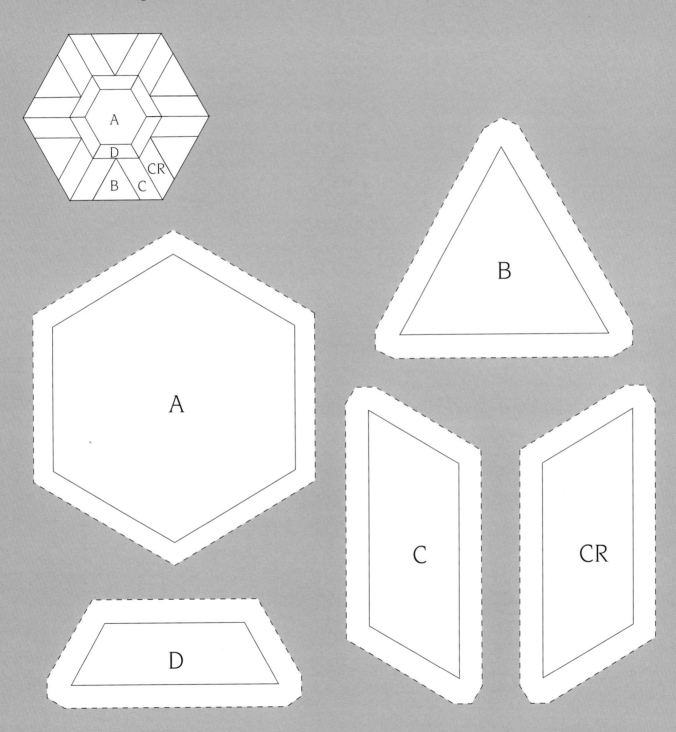

Diamonds and Arrow Points block. Made by Ruby Downing, Oak Grove, Missouri.

the 1945 diamonds and arrow points

Published February 21, 1945

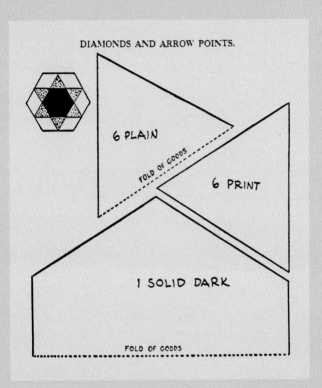

DIAMONDS AND ARROW POINTS.

6 PLAIN

FOLD OF GOODS

6 PRINT

1 SOLID DARK

FOLD OF GOODS

"This geometric figure affords opportunity for very pleasing effect with alternate rows of plain and print blocks. The design is one from the store of Hazel Mullinax, Stuart, OK."
-The Kansas City Star

*February 21, 1945, in The Star...*3,650 U.S. soldiers are reported killed in fighting at Iwo Jima. ● Gen. George Patton pushed his armored division into the heart of Nazi Germany. ● A new sign is placed on Harry Truman's Washington office. The old sign read "The Hon. Harry Truman" the new sign read "The Vice President Harry Truman."

cutting and piecing
the 1945 diamonds and arrows points

Block size
9 inches

Fabrics needed
light, medium prints and dark.

Cut
from light fabric, cut six diamonds
using **template C.**

Cut
from medium prints, cut six triangles
using **template B.**

Cut
from dark fabric, cut one hexagon
using **template A.**

Note
It is recommended that all seam
lines be marked for accuracy.

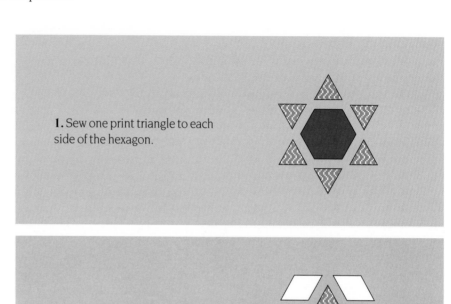

1. Sew one print triangle to each
side of the hexagon.

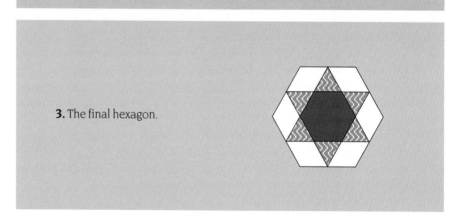

2. Inset a light diamond between
each star point to finish the block.

3. The final hexagon.

Quilter's wisdom

"To make many points come together, (for example, when making a six-pointed star) use the "spider web" technique.
Run your needle diagonally from one connecting point to the next. Go through each piece that meets. This will
draw every piece together making all the points match." -*Edie McGinnis*

quilting templates for
the 1945 diamonds and arrows points

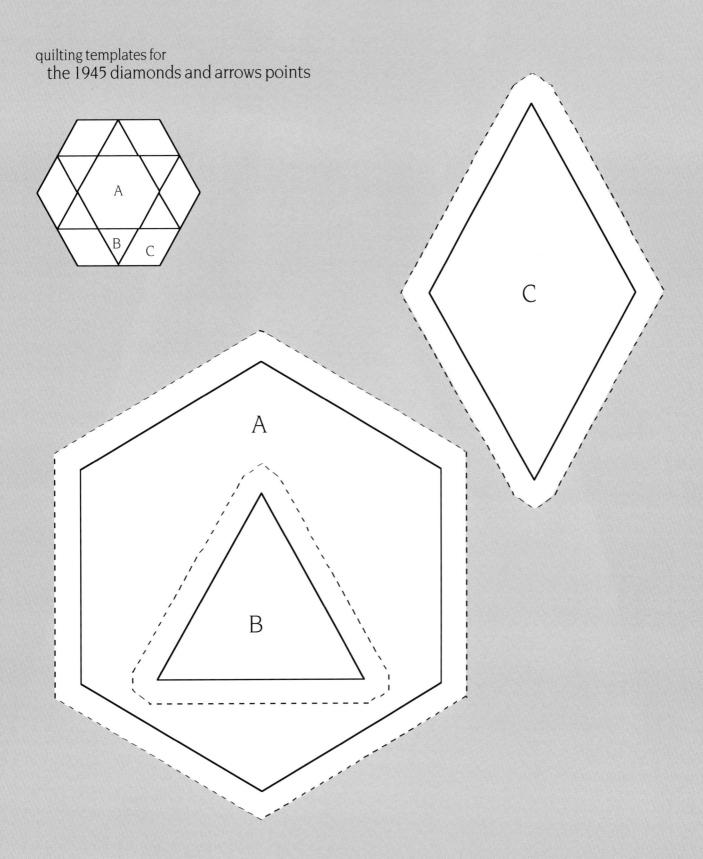

Ozark Star.
Pieced by Lena Minden.
Owned by Vera Minden Kaiser

the 1935 ozark star

"This quilt was on my dad's bed when he passed away. I don't remember it as a child so I think my parents got it from my paternal grandmother, Lena Minden, after I got married. Both my grandmothers quilted and I learned very young.

"I really like this Ozark Star and, judging from the fabric, think it was made in the 30's or 40's. We always cut the quilt patterns out of *The Star* and *Weekly Star Farmer*. As a child I made a sickle quilt from a Star pattern but used it up when I married, as it was the only cover we had. I later made another to replace it.

"The quilting is very nice on this quilt. It was probably quilted by some of my aunts. This quilt was documented in the Kansas Quilt Project 1986 and is marked so on the back." *-Vera Minden Kaiser, Paola, Kansas*

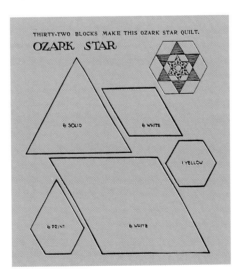

Published December 18, 1935

*That day in The Star...*Italian dictator Benito Mussolini threatened Europe with war, rejecting French and British peace proposals. ● Local Democrats objected to a $10 a plate ticket price for a Jackson Day banquet and fundraiser. ● Four female garment workers were arrested in Kansas City for calling an illegal strike against the Reiter and Levin Coat Company.

cutting and piecing
the 1935 ozark star

Block size
9 inches

Fabrics needed
light, assorted prints and dark.

Cut
from light fabric, cut one hexagon using **template A**, six diamonds using **template D** and six diamonds using **template B**.

Cut
from the assorted prints, cut six-petals using **template C**.

Cut
from the dark fabric, cut six triangles using **template E**.

Note
It is recommended that all seam lines be marked for accuracy.

1. Sew the print petals onto the center hexagon leaving the side seams open. When all the petals are sewn on, go back and sew the side seams closed.

2. Inset light (D) diamonds between the points of the petals forming a hexagon.

4. Inset light (B) diamonds between the star points to complete the block.

3. Add dark (E) triangles to this hexagon forming another star.

5. The final hexagon block.

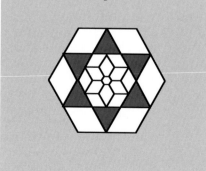

Quilter's wisdom

"If you prick your finger and bleed on your quilt block while sewing, the best thing to remove the blood is with your own saliva. -*Mary Ellen Bloomquist*

quilting templates for
the 1935 ozark star

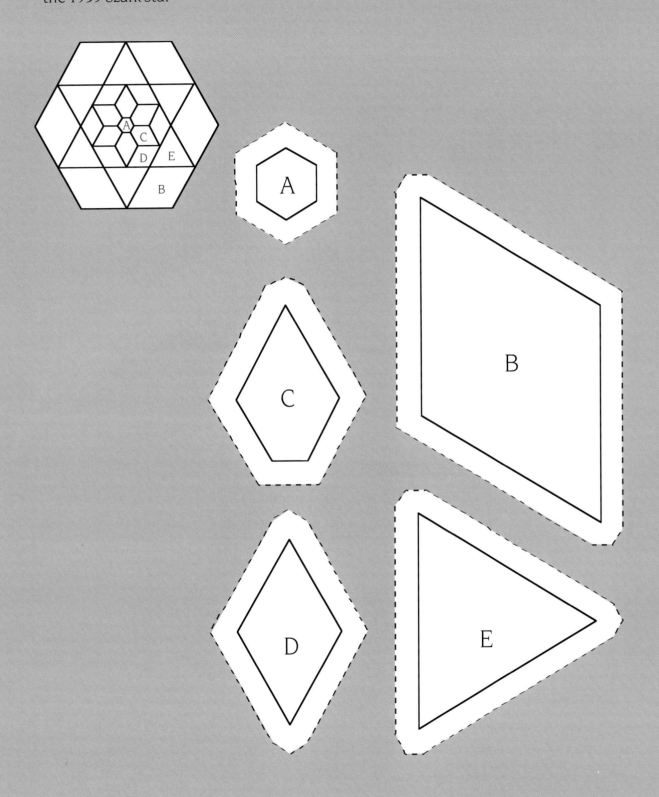

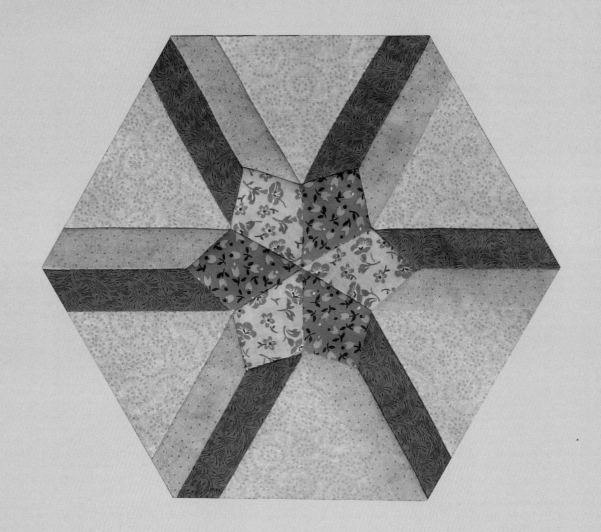

From a Grandmother's Collection block. Made by Edie McGinnis, Kansas City, Missouri.

the 1959 from a grandmother's collection

Published August 19, 1959

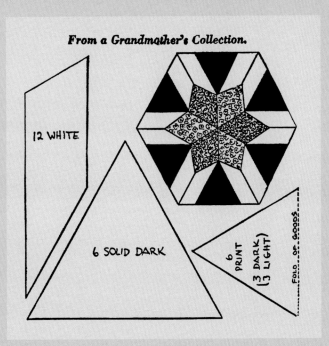

"In her grandmother's day, writes Mrs. Thomas Booker of Perry, Mo., this quilt block was named 'Mother's Prayers.' Its several geometrical parts offer a choice of various contrasting one-tone combinations and a small print for the star figure." -*The Kansas City Star*

August 19, 1959, in The Star...Eight people were reported dead in an earthquake in southwest Montana. ● Two fire fighters died battling a blaze on Southwest Boulevard. ● The musical comedy "Li'l Abner" opened at the Starlight Theater.

cutting and piecing
the 1959 from a grandmother's collection

Block size
9 inches

Fabrics needed
light, medium light, a dark and two contrasting prints

Cut
from the light fabric: Cut 12 print diamonds with **template A.**

Cut
from medium light fabric, cut six parallelograms using **template B.** When cutting these pieces, make sure your fabric is layered rather than folded. If it is folded, half of the pieces will be reversed and will not work.

Cut
from each of the prints, cut three diamonds using **template C.**

Cut
from dark fabric, cut six parallelograms using **template BR.** Again, make sure your fabric is layered rather than folded.

Note
It is recommended that all seam lines be marked for accuracy.

Quilter's wisdom
"If it doesn't fit, cut it off." -Lois Frost

1. Sew three diamonds together alternating prints, thereby making one half of the center star.

2. Sew the other three diamonds together, again alternating prints, making the other half of the star. Sew the two halves together.

3. Sew a (B) parallelogram to a light (A) triangle. Sew a (BR) parallelogram to the triangle. You will have a unit that looks like this:

Sew the remaining triangles and parallelograms together in the same manner.

4. Sew the triangular units to the center star, leaving the side seams open.

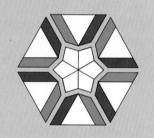

5. After all triangular units are sewn to the center star, sew the side seams. This will make the final hexagon block.

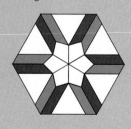

quilting templates for
the 1959 from a grandmother's collection

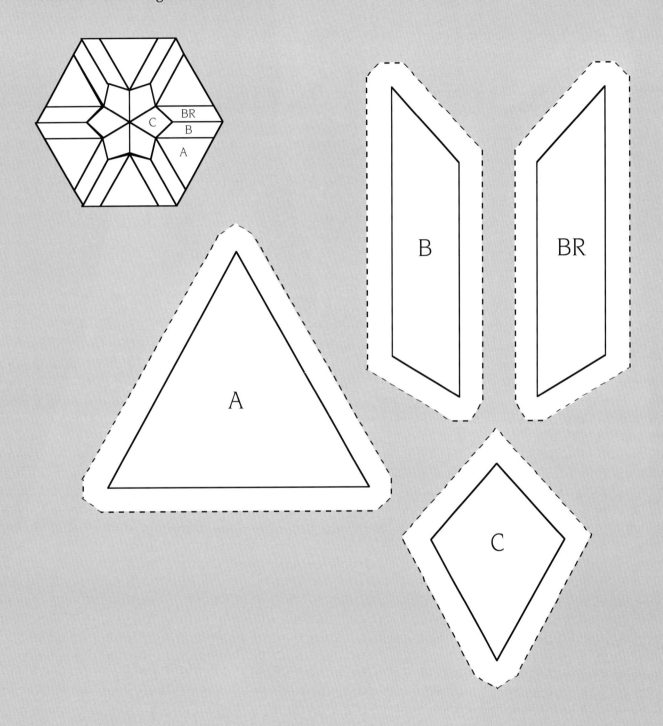

Boutonniere.
Owned by Joyce Savage.

the 1931 boutonniere

"This quilt was made by my grandmother, Helen Rychlec, in the early 1930s. My mother, Theresa Monchil, remembers her mother making quilts with four or five other ladies in the neighborhood (Kansas City, Kan.). My mom said the ladies would all bring pieces of scrap materials they had left over from dresses and shirts they made for their husbands and children. My grandmother also sewed aprons, which she sold throughout the neighborhood. Many of the scraps from these were also included in the quilt. My mother remembers them trading material. She also remembers them getting together in the afternoon to quilt the quilt. They would all go to a room upstairs and sit around the quilt which was anchored to two long poles. While they were quilting they would talk up a storm in Polish. My mother doesn't know what they were saying, but she remembers that they never ran out of words.

"When the quilts were done, my mother, her brothers and her sisters would try to find pieces in it from their shirts and dresses. Everyone got excited when they found a piece of their clothing in the quilt.

"Many of the quilts were made for the neighborhood ladies or given as Christmas gifts to other family members."-*Joyce Savage*

Published September 26, 1931
That day in The Star...Col. Charles Lindbergh flew to Nanking, China, with a plane load of medical supplies and was mobbed by a desperately hungry crowd. ● Despite pleas from the British, Mahatma Gandhi continued to lead India in a boycott of foreign cotton goods. ● A stray bullet injured two men when it crashed through their car window as they waited at a traffic signal at the corner of Seventh and Washington in Kansas City, Kansas.

cutting and piecing
the 1931 boutonniere

Block size
9 inches

Fabrics needed
light, assorted scrap prints and a dark.

Cut
from light fabric, cut one hexagon using **template A**.

Cut
from prints, cut six petals using **template B**.

Cut
from dark fabric, cut six diamonds using **template C**.

Note
It is recommended that all seam lines be marked for accuracy.

1. Sew the print petals to the center hexagon leaving the side seams open. After all the petals have been sewn on, sew the side seams closed.

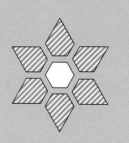

2. Inset a dark diamond between each petal finishing the block into a hexagon.

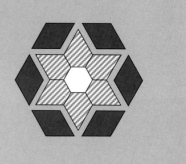

3. The final hexagon.

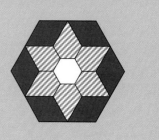

Quilter's wisdom

"Don't get too wrapped up in how many projects you begin or how much fabric you own. Enjoy the process and you have accomplished the important part." -*Jerry Stube*

quilting templates for
the 1931 boutonniere

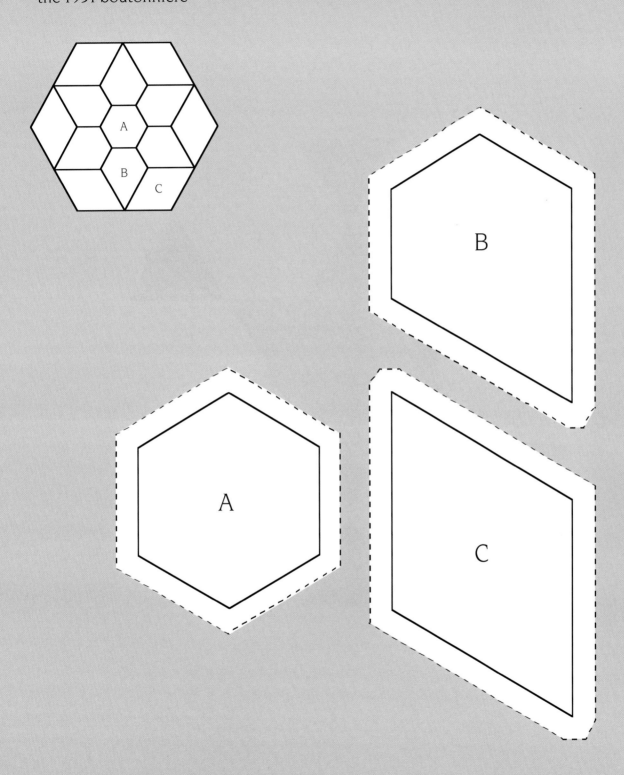

The Hexagon Star block. Made by Sharon McMillan, Marquette Heights, Illinois.

the 1940 hexagon star

Published October 9, 1940

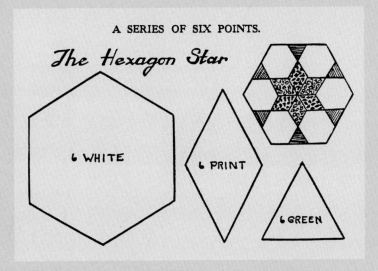

"This 6-pointed star surrounded by hexagons that are separated by triangular insets is a design of Mrs. Jesse Parker, rural route No. 1, Minco, OK. She prefers the sections of the star of print, the hexagon of 1-tone material and the triangles or half-diamonds of contrasting 1-tone fabric." -*The Kansas City Star*

October 9, 1940, in The Star...Nazi warplanes continued bombing England, killing hundreds in London hospitals. ● A poll predicted that Republican Wendall Wilkie would be elected president with a minimum of 334 electoral votes. ● 10,000 Episcopalians gathered in Kansas City for their 53rd triennial convention.

cutting and piecing
the 1940 hexagon star

Block size
9 inches

Fabrics needed
light and dark.

Cut
from light fabric, cut six hexagons
using **template A**.

Cut
from dark fabric, cut six diamonds
using **template B** and six triangles
using **template C**.

Note
It is recommended that all seam
lines be marked for accuracy.

1. Sew three (B) diamonds
together to form one half of the
center star.

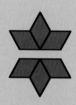

2. Sew the other three (B)
diamonds together to form the
other half of the star. Sew the two
star halves together.

3. To three of the hexagons, add
two (C) triangles making units
that look like this.

4. Then add a hexagon unit.
Continue in this manner until the
block is finished.

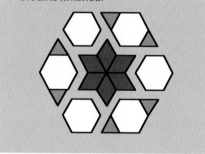

5. The final hexagon block.

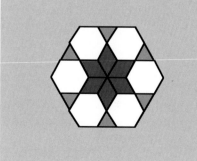

Quilter's wisdom

"When washing fat quarters, wash and dry them in a lingerie bag."
-Bonnie Lindsay

quilting templates for
the 1940 hexagon star

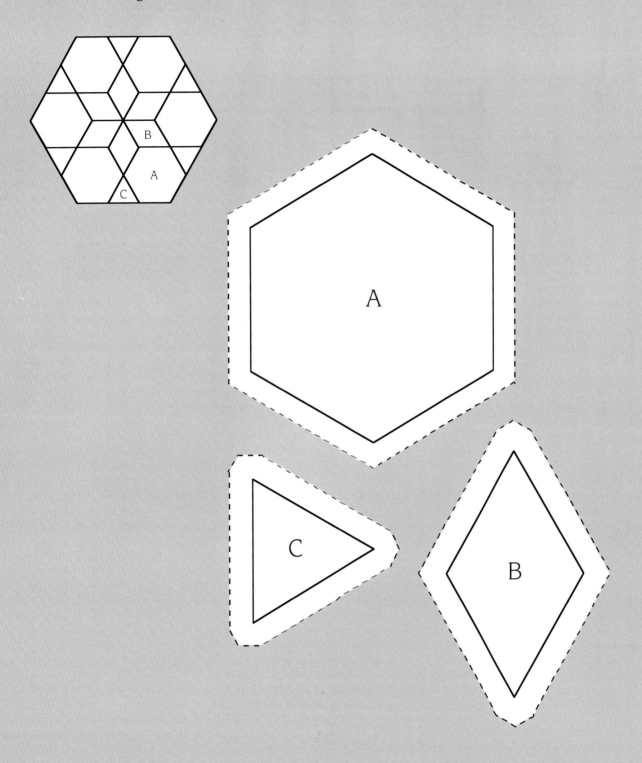

Pin Wheel.
Owned by Judy Streu,
Liberty, Missouri.

the 1934 pinwheel

"The Pinwheel quilt, as sketched today was what originated when Mrs. Charles P. Newton, Denison, Tex. gave her 11-year-old daughter Mary some scraps to make a little quilt. Once making the design she sewed nineteen of the blocks together to make a pillow cover. Allow for seams." -*The Kansas City Star*

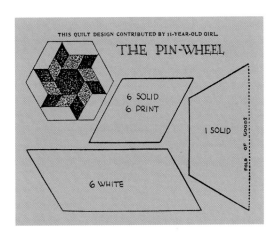

Published April 7, 1934

*That day in The Star...*Outlaw Clyde Barrow released an Oklahoma police chief that he had held hostage, bragging that he and his companion Bonnie Parker were "too smart to be captured." ● 50 people were reported dead in Norway following a seaside rock slide and subsequent flooding. ● A new "streamlined, high-speed" train operated by Union Pacific railroad was shown off at Union Station in Kansas City.

cutting and piecing
the 1934 pinwheel

Block size
9 inches

Fabrics needed
light, medium and dark

Cut
from light fabric, cut one hexagon using **template A** and six parallelograms using **template B**. Make sure your fabric is layered, rather than folded. If the fabric is folded, half of the pieces will be reversed and will not work.

Cut
from medium fabric, cut six diamonds using **template C**.

Cut
from dark fabric, cut six diamonds using **template C**.

Note
It is recommended that all seam lines be marked for accuracy.

Quilter's wisdom
"When threading your needle, wet the eye of the needle, not the thread. The thread will then go through the eye of the needle quite smoothly." -*Helen Johnson*

1. Sew a medium diamond to a dark diamond to make a unit. Make six of these units.

2. Sew the medium part of the unit to the center hexagon as shown. This leaves the dark diamond dangling for the moment.

3. Going counterclockwise, sew the units around the hexagon. Sew the last unit on and close up the seam of the dangling diamond.

4. Inset the parallelograms to complete the block.

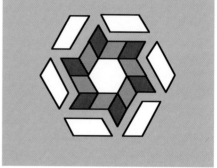

5. The final hexagon block.

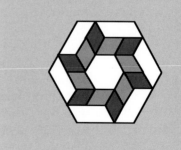

quilting templates for
the 1934 pinwheel

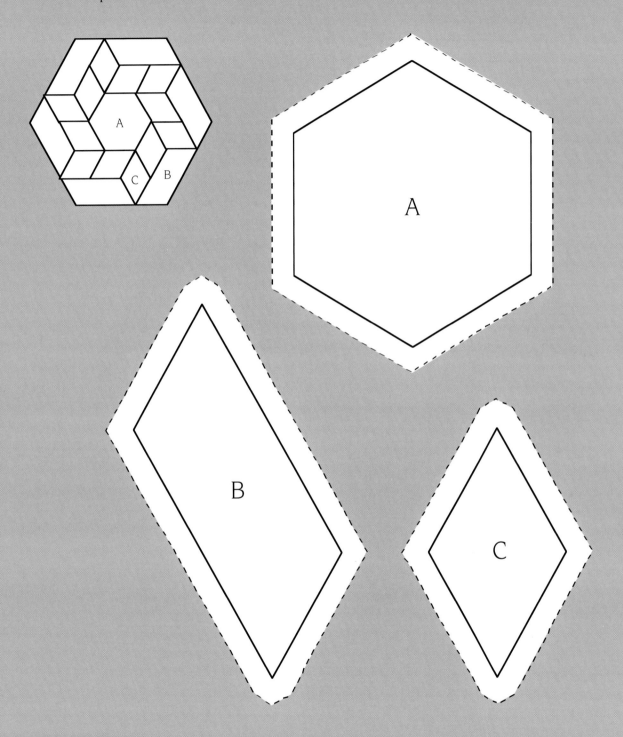

A

B

C

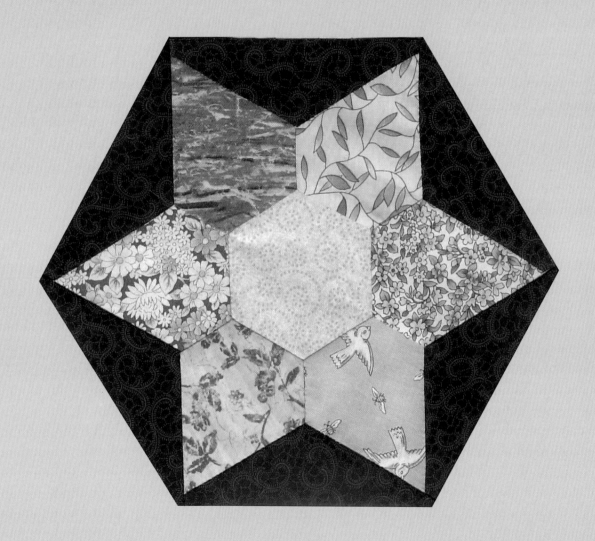

Six-Point Flower Garden block. Made by Rosemary Garten, Independence, Missouri.

the 1959 six-pointed flower garden

Published July 22, 1959

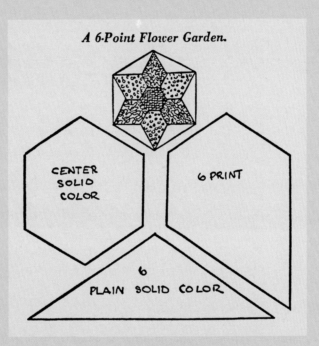

"The flower garden block suggests dainty small pieces for the points with contrast for the border in the way of a checked or striped piece. Another thought is to make the center block of the same material chosen for the one-tone border pieces." *-The Kansas City Star*

*July 22, 1959, in The Star...*The G.I. Bill was approved by the U.S. Senate. ● The United States navy ordered all of its ships patrolling within range of Communist countries to have their guns loaded and positioned to fire. ● Kansas City's Barbara Stell competed against 14 other young women in the Miss U.S.A. pageant in Long Beach, California.

cutting and piecing
the 1959 six-pointed flower garden

Block size
9 inches

Fabrics needed
light, assorted prints and dark.

Cut
from light fabric cut center hexagon using **template A.**

Cut
from prints, cut six flower petals using **template B.**

Cut
from dark fabric, cut six triangles using **template C.**

Note
It is recommended that all seam lines be marked for accuracy.

1. Sew petals to center hexagon leaving side seams open. After all petals are sewn to center hexagon, sew the side seams together.

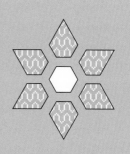

2. Inset dark triangles between petal points to finish the block.

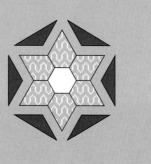

3. The final hexagon.

Quilter's wisdom

"To quickly take out machine stitches, use your seam ripper to cut (or clip) every third or fourth stitch. Turn your work over and slip the seam ripper under the thread. The whole row will lift right off!" -*Shirley Duncan*

quilting templates for
the 1959 six-pointed flower garden

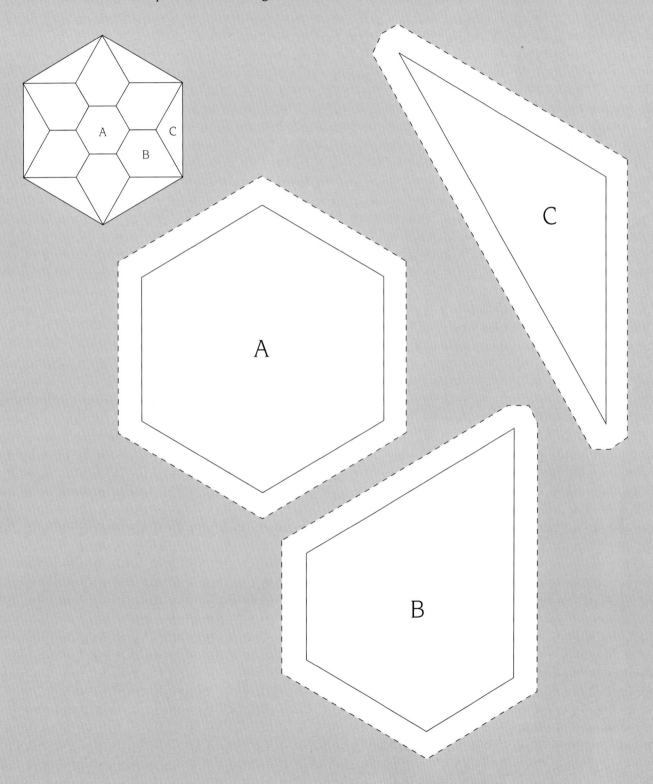

Oklahoma Star.
Owned by Reylene Harbit,
Warrensburg, Missouri

the 1945 oklahoma star

"This was made by my husband's mother, Evalena Harbit, who died before we were married. It was made when she was in her eighties. I was so happy that it was given to me. I felt really special." -*Reylene Harbit, Warrensburg, Missouri*

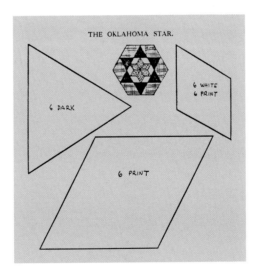

Published January 17, 1945

*That day in The Star...*The Nazi siege of Warsaw ended as Soviet troops liberated the city. ● 300 American warplanes bombed Japanese-occupied Hong Kong and Formosa. ● A newly built about-to-open grocery store on Euclid Avenue in Kansas City was destroyed by fire and looted by onlookers.

cutting and piecing
the 1945 oklahoma star

Block size
9 inches

Fabrics needed
light, medium prints and dark.

Cut
from light fabric, cut six diamonds using **template B** and six diamonds using **template A**.

Cut
from medium prints, cut six diamonds using **template A**.

Cut
from dark fabric, cut six triangles using **template C**.

Note
It is recommended that all seam lines be marked for accuracy.

1. Sew three of the print diamonds (A) together to form one half of the center star.

2. Sew the other three print diamonds together to form the other half of the star. Sew the two halves together.

3. Inset light diamonds between the star points forming a hexagon.

4. Sew six dark triangles (C) on the star points, as shown.

5. Inset the light (B) diamonds to finish the block.

6. The final hexagon block.

Quilter's wisdom
"Always share what you learn with others." *-Toni Steere*

quilting templates for
the 1945 oklahoma star

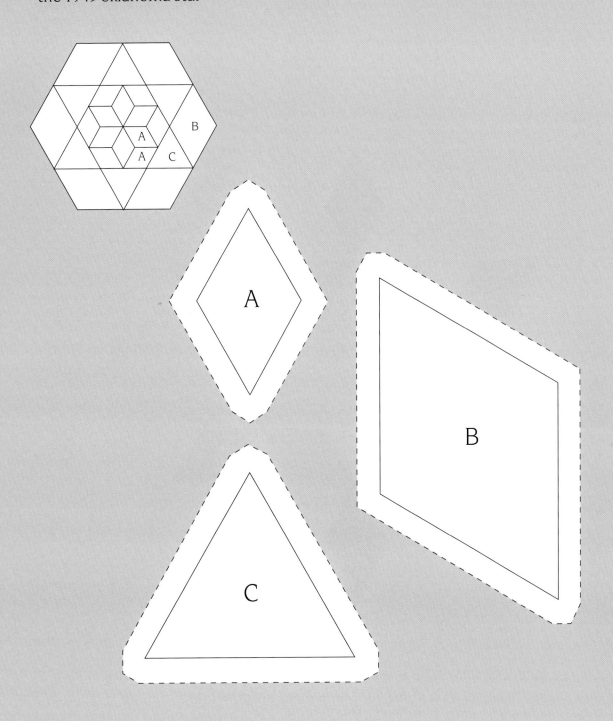

Ozark Diamond block. Made by Sue McNamara of Peoria, Illinois.

the 1931 ozark diamond

Published June 20, 1931

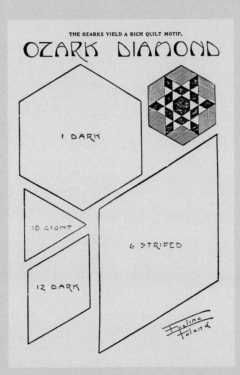

"Hexagons, triangles and diamonds go together to make this 'Ozark Diamond' block one of the most fascinating printed for a long time. It is one in which the ingenuity of the quilter may be put to effective use for there are an unusually large number of combinations possible. Light and dark fabric combined with striped or flowered materials are suggestions. No seams are allowed." -*The Kansas City Star*

*June 20, 1931, in The Star...*Kansas City celebrated its "Jubilee" with concerts, air shows, parades, water frolics, rodeos, and fireworks. ● In a move to ease the worldwide Depression, President Herbert Hoover called for a moratorium on all debts and reparations from World War I. ● Kansas City and the rest of the Midwest was suffering through a heat wave that killed twelve people in Chicago.

cutting and piecing
the 1931 ozark diamond

Block size
9 inches

Fabrics needed
light, medium and dark.

Cut
from light fabric, cut center hexagon using **template A** and six diamonds using **template B**.

Cut
from medium fabric, cut eighteen triangles using **template C**.

Cut
from dark fabric, cut twelve diamonds using **template D**.

Note
It is recommended that all seam lines be marked for accuracy.

1. Make six **A Unit** sections as follows: Sew a (C) triangle to two sides of a (D) diamond. The unit will look like this:

Set these units aside.

2. Sew a (C) triangle to each side of the center hexagon.

3. Inset a (D) diamond between each star point.

4. Next sew an **A Unit** onto each side of the hexagon.

5. Inset large (B) diamonds to finish the block.

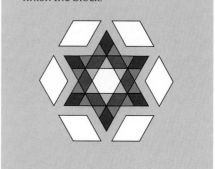

6. The final hexagon block.

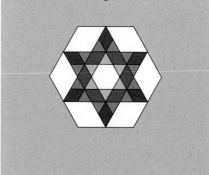

Quilter's wisdom
"Learn to quilt from a quilt shop that shows you the 'shortcuts.'"
-Joanne Scolari, Twin Falls, Idaho

quilting templates for
the 1931 ozark diamond

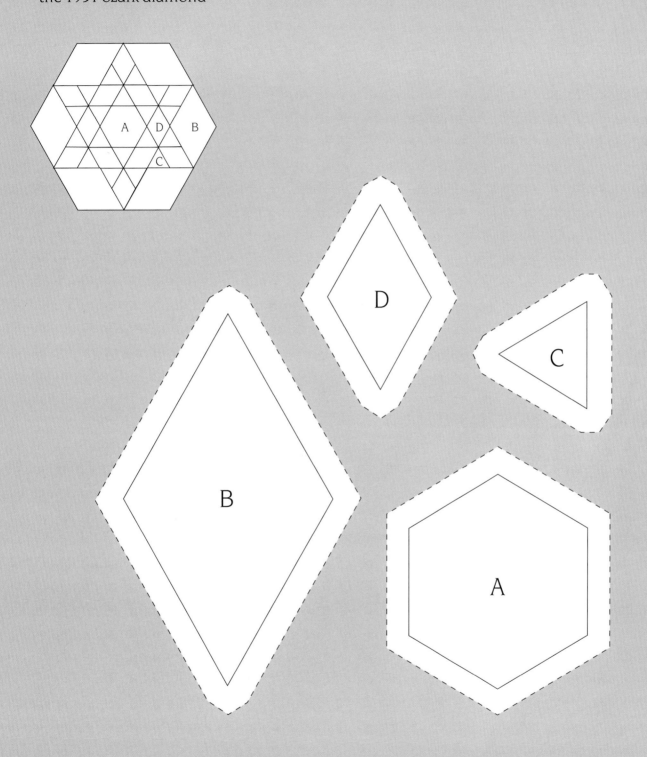

the 1936 pointing star

Left, facing page.
Pointing Star.
Owned by Rita Smith,
Holt, Missouri

"This quilt was made by my husband's mother and grandmother. It is the last one they both worked on in the late 30s to early 40s. The piecing has all been done by hand and is made of flour sacks. That's all the fabric they had at the time. This quilt top is a family heirloom that I plan to finish with the help of my daughter and granddaughter. Five generations of our family will have worked on it by the time it is quilted."
-Rita Smith, Holt, Missouri

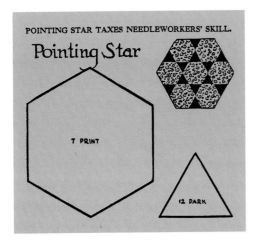

Published March 21, 1936
*That day in The Star...*Floods in Ohio and New England claim the lives of 168 people. ● Italian warplanes drop mustard gas bombs on civilian targets in Ethiopia. ● Kansas City detective chief Thomas Higgins ordered the arrest of all drug "peddlers" and addicts on the city's streets.

cutting and piecing
the 1936 pointing star

Block size
9 inches

Fabrics needed
light and dark.

Cut
from dark fabric, cut twelve triangles using **template A.**

Cut
from light fabric, cut seven hexagons using **template B.**

Note
It is recommended that all seam lines be marked for accuracy.

1. Sew two (A) triangles to (B) hexagon as shown to make one **A Unit.** Make three units total.

2. Sew two triangles (A) to a hexagon (B), as shown. Make two such **B Units.**

4. Sew the second row together by adding triangles to hexagons. Sew the three rows together.

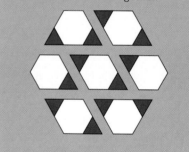

3. Sew one **A Unit** to one **B Unit** to make the top row, as shown. Repeat to make the bottom row.

5. The final hexagon.

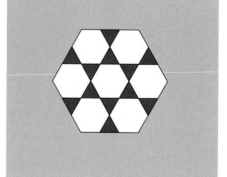

Quilter's wisdom
"Preplan your pressing. Pressing towards the dark fabric is not always the best. You should always press in the direction that will give you the least amount of resistance when you butt your seams together."
-*Linda Kreisel*

quilting templates for
the 1936 pointing star

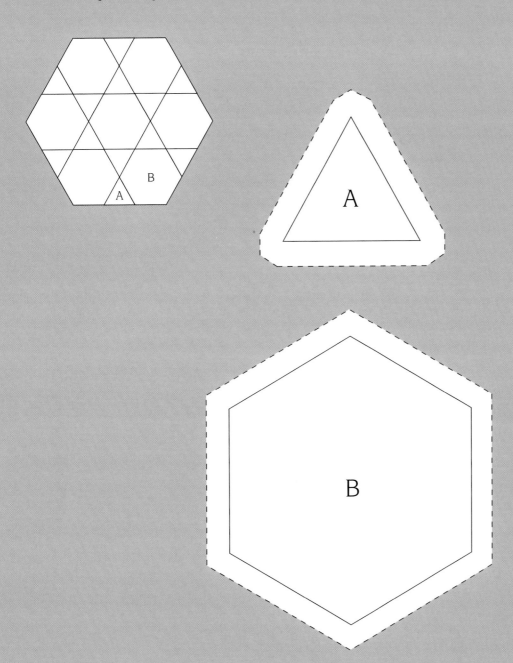

B

A

A

B

Pointing Star.
Owned by Katherine Stanley,
Centerville, Kansas.

the quilter's gallery

"My Aunt Willa pieced and quilted this quilt using fabrics of my mother's dresses. It is a treasured memory of these two women." -*Rosemary Warren Cromer*

Boutonniere. Owned by Rosemary Warren Cromer, Overland Park, Kansas.

Top left, clockwise: The Pinwheel block. Made by Peggy McFeeters of Morton, Illinois. Oklahoma Star block. Made by Alta Short of Independence, Missouri. Hidden Star block. Made by Sue McNamara of Peoria, Illinois. Floating Clouds block. Made by Donna English of Independence, Missouri.

Left, facing page. Pinwheel. Owned by Judy Streu, Liberty, Missouri.

Oklahoma Star.
Owned by Florence Bessmer,
Buckner, Missouri

putting it all together

Hexagon blocks.

Now that we have made our twenty blocks, it is time to put them all together. Since our blocks are not very large, we can add to the height and width of the quilt simply by making more than one of each block or by adding blank accent hexagons, triangles or 60-degree diamonds (the templates of which are provided on the following pages).

figure 1.

figure 2.

In figure 1, pieced blocks are alternated with accent blocks. The blocks are sewn together with some rows ending in half-blocks depending on the width of the quilt.

When making half-blocks you cannot just cut a block in half. You must physically construct the half-block. This will assure having seam allowances on the ends, therefore, the side or top of your quilt will have a straight edge. The straight edge will enable you to bind your quilt efficiently and/or allow you to add a border for increased height or width. As you can see in the illustration, row 2 is offset and inset into row 1.

figure 2.

figure 1.

To inset a seam

Make sure all seams are marked. Match up the corner of the piece to be set in with the corner of the piece to which it is to be sewn. Pin at the beginning and the end of the seam and sew, being careful not to sew beyond the marked seamline. Realign the pieces and pin the piece to be sewn from corner to corner. Sew the seam from the inside corner to the outside corner ending at the marked seam line and press.

In figure 2, the pieced blocks alternate with accent blocks. When using this type of setting, there is no need to use half-blocks. The blocks are separated from each other by using equilateral triangles at the top and bottom of the quilt and 9-inch 60-degree diamonds on the rest of the rows. This setting is easily constructed by sewing rows together vertically rather than horizontally.

Sew a pieced block to an accent block until the quilt is the length desired. Sew an equilateral triangle to the first hexagon block in the row. Then inset a diamond between each hexagon block and finish the row with another triangle. Continue in this manner until you have the width needed for the quilt. The top and bottom of the quilt will have nice straight edges and the sides will have a lovely scalloped edge, which is easy to bind.

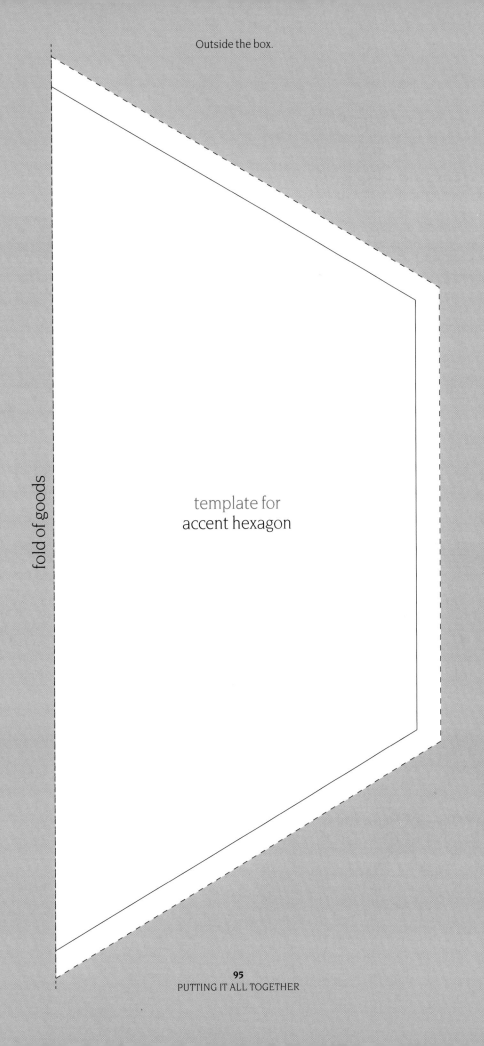

Outside the box.

fold of goods

template for
accent hexagon

figure 3, 3a, 3b and 3c.

In figure 3, the pieced blocks are set together using equilateral triangles. Every other row is offset from the previous row. A secondary pattern of a six-pointed star is created in the background of the quilt when the triangle is used.

For row 1, sew a triangle to a half-block as shown in Figure 3a. To a full block sew two triangles as shown in Figure 3b. Continue to the end of the row in this manner finishing with another half block.

For the second row add triangles as shown in Figure 3c. Trim off the excess edges of the triangles on each end of this row.

Continue in this manner, alternating rows until your quilt is the desired size. Since each edge of the quilt comes out straight, you can add borders to increase the dimensions of the finished quilt.

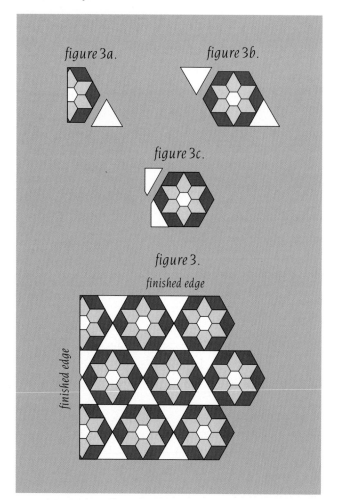

figure 3a.

figure 3b.

figure 3c.

figure 3.

finished edge

finished edge

figure 4.

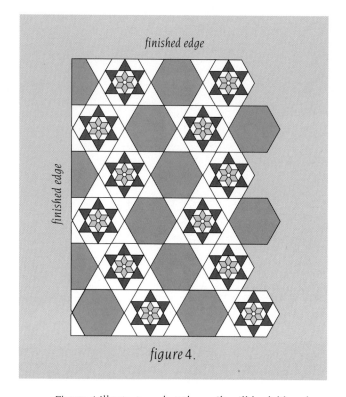

finished edge

finished edge

figure 4.

Figure 4 illustrates what the quilt will look like when using the triangles, a pieced block and an accent block. As you can see, the background star still pops out making a striking setting for the blocks.

After the top is finished, it is time to add the backing and the batting. Here's where a little or a lot of help from your friends is priceless. Mark the exact center of the quilt backing on the sides and the ends with a straight pin. Lay the backing, wrong side up, on a flat surface and anchor it by taping it down or clipping it to a table top with large binder clips, making sure there are no wrinkles or creases in the backing. Lay the batting on top of the backing centering it as closely as possible. Mark the exact center of the top, horizontally and vertically with pins, just as you did the backing. Lay the quilt top, face up, on top of the batting. Match up the pins on the top and the backing as closely as possible and clip the three layers together. Baste the three layers together and quilt.

After the quilting is finished, trim the backing and the batting to match the top and bind. It is recommended that bias binding be used when the quilt edges are not straight. Bias binding can be purchased ready-made or can be made by the quilter.

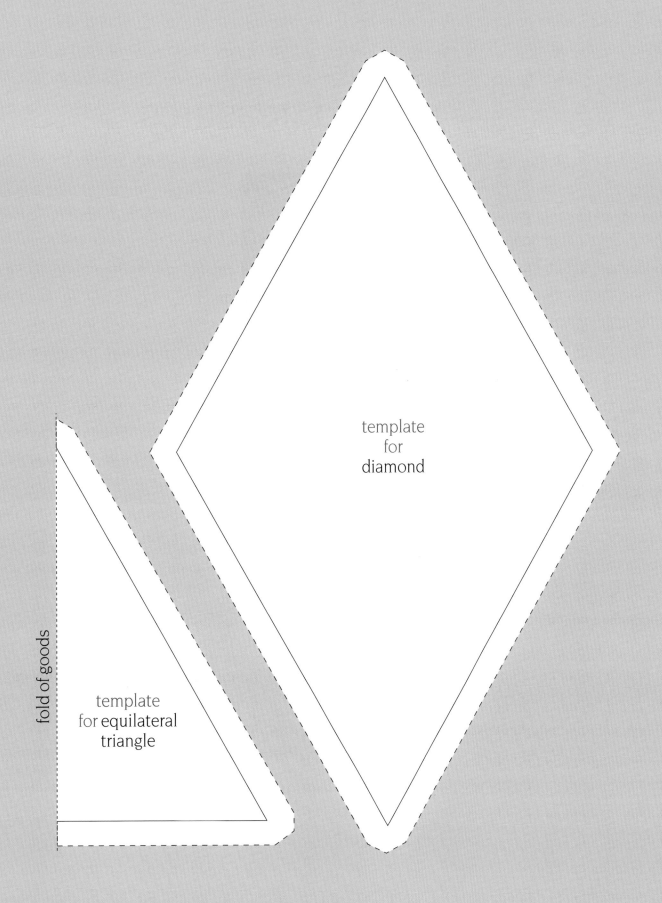

template
for
diamond

fold of goods

template
for equilateral
triangle

taking care of quilted treasures

by Edie McGinnis

When people find out that I'm a quilter, they often share their memories of their mother, grandmother, or aunt, who was also a quilter. Some people have been fortunate enough to inherit quilts from these relatives. They assure me that they are taking good care of their quilt. They've wrapped it in a plastic bag and put in a nice dark place where the sunlight won't get to it. This is where I start to cringe in pity for the poor quilt.

This is also where I have the opportunity to educate people about how to be kind to their quilt. First and foremost, never, ever store a quilt in plastic. Plastic collects moisture from humidity in the air. The dampness and the heat from the plastic will cause mildew to form on the fabric and can also rot the thread and fabric. The best way to store a quilt is to lay it out flat on an extra bed. If you have more than one quilt, put them on top of one another on the bed. Cover the bed with an old sheet or coverlet since both sunlight and natural light will make the fabric fade.

If you don't have an extra bed on which to lay your quilt, the next best thing to do is to fold it using acid free tissue paper in the folds. Then store it wrapped in a sheet or pillowcase. The fabric wrapper will keep the light away and keep the quilt from touching any undesirable surface such as wood on a shelf, while allowing the fabric in the quilt to breathe.

If your quilt smells even slightly musty, lay it on a sheet outside on the ground and let it air out. The sunshine will kill many odors that fabric picks up. Be sure you anchor both the sheet and the quilt so they don't blow away.

If you must wash your quilt, wash it gently in a soap that is recommended specifically for antique fabrics. Put water and soap in the bathtub and swish it around to mix it up. Add your quilt. Let it soak for a while. Then let the water out of the tub and press the soapy water out of the quilt. Do not wring the quilt. Run clear water into the tub as many times as needed to rinse the soapy water out of the quilt. You can make this task easier by not using much soap in the first place.

After rinsing, lay a clean sheet on the ground, anchoring the corners. Lay the wet quilt on the sheet and let it dry. Turn the quilt several times during the course of the day to aid the drying

Boutonniere. Made and owned by Zella Johnson, Independence, Missouri.

process. This is better than using a clothesline. When a quilt is draped across a clothesline, there is a great deal of stress on the seams and threads in the fabric of the quilt.

If you use an automatic dryer, use the delicate fabric setting and set the temperature on air dry. It will take quite awhile to dry this way but the quilt will escape the harsh effects of a very hot dryer.

If you actually use your quilt on your bed or to wrap up in on a cold day, (that's what they were intended for, after all) it will get worn along the binding or the fabric in some of the patchwork will wear out or become thin and fragile. Sometimes it's the kids or the pets that will damage a quilt. In any case, make repairs as soon as possible. If your quilt has a piece that needs to be replaced, cut out a piece of fabric that is a bit larger and shaped the same as the piece you are repairing. Hopefully you can find fabric of the same vintage and close to the same color. Pin the piece over the patchwork on the quilt. Turn the edge under and applique (sew over) to the quilt. Sew all around the new piece with tiny stitches. Be patient. If it doesn't look good the first time, take the new piece off and try again. It's worth the time and effort to do a good job here. If you are uncertain of your ability to repair the quilt, ask for guidance at your local quilt shop.

If the dog chews the center out of your quilt, you might consider it a lost cause. I actually heard of a person to whom this happened. The story goes that she refrained from killing the dog and made a new center for her quilt that contained a picture of the dog. I expect that eliminated a lot of explaining. I'm not so sure the dog would have fared so well at my house. Sometimes it's necessary to be especially creative when it comes to repairs. A nice applique is usually the answer to an unsightly tear caused by a pet or a cut inflicted by your two-year-old who has snitched your scissors.

If the binding is frayed and needs to be replaced, take the old binding off. Select a color of fabric that is in the quilt top and match it as closely as possible. Make the new binding and sew it in place.

I must admit that one of my quilts has a lovely applique butterfly on one of the borders. One of my sons was writing with a red magic marker on my bed and kind of ran off the edge of the paper and onto my quilt.

Of course the marker was the permanent kind. Now that he is grown and gone from home, I run my fingers over that butterfly and remember him as a little boy.

glossary

Background (or secondary) fabric: A secondary fabric that complements the predominant fabric used in a quilt. (See also primary fabric.)

Backing: The bottom layer of a quilt.

Baste: Pinning or loosely stitching layers of a quilt together in preparation for quilting. The pins or stitches are later removed and the quilting holds all the layers of the quilt together.

Batting: The middle layer of the quilt, which provides depth and warmth. Batting, mainly cotton or polyester, is sold in lofts; a high loft is thick, a low loft is thin. The thinner the loft, the easier it is to quilt.

Binding: A strip of fabric used to enclose the rough edges of all the layers of a finished quilt.

Block: A square unit consisting of pieces of fabric sewn into a design. Many blocks sewn together make a quilt top.

Piecing: Stitching together quilt pieces.

Press to, press away: To iron the fabric in a block. "Press to dark" means iron both sides of the seam toward the darker fabric; "press to the edge" means iron both sides of the seam toward the outer edge of the fabric, and so on. "Press away" means the opposite, as in "press away from center."

Primary fabric: The predominant fabric used in a quilt.

Quilting: Stitching through the top, middle and bottom layers of a quilt in a design or in straight lines to secure the layers together and add a decorative touch.

Quilting hoop: A two-part wooden or plastic circle. Placed on either side of the quilt, the hoop holds the fabric taut inside.

Quilting needles: Smaller than sewing needles, quilting needles are called "betweens." They come in sizes from 7 (longest) to 12 (shortest). Beginning quilters often use a 7 or 8.

Quilting thimble: A thimble with a ridge around the top to help push the quilting needle.

Quilting thread: Heavier and stronger than average sewing thread.

Right side: The front side of the fabric with a pattern or color; the opposite of the "wrong side," or back of a fabric.

Running stitch: A sewing stitch made by passing the needle in and out repeatedly, using short, even stitches.

Selvages: The lengthwise, finished edges of a fabric.

Seams: The line formed by sewing together pieces of fabric.

Seam guide: A mark or piece on a sewing machine footplate that measures the distance from the needle to the edge of the fabric.

Template: A pattern, usually plastic, used to trace cutting or sewing lines onto fabric.

Wrong side: See Right side.

Boutonniere.
Owned by Marilyn Zerwekh,
Lawrence, Kansas.

star quilts: year by year

Here is a chronological list –including repeats – of the quilt patterns and designs published by The Kansas City Star from 1928 through 1961.

If you'd like to see the patterns on the pages of the newspaper, microfilm copies of The Star are available at the Kansas City Public Library's Main Branch, 311 East 12th Street, Kansas City, Missouri.

For an alphabetical list of the designs, see Wilene Smith's Quilt Patterns: An Index to The Kansas City Star Patterns (details in Bibliography).

For a thumbnail sketch of each pattern, see Volume 5 of The Ultimate Illustrated Index to The Kansas City Star Quilt Pattern Collection by the Central Oklahoma Quilters Guild (details in Bibliography).

Months not listed here had no published quilt patterns.

SEPTEMBER 1928
Pine Tree
Album Quilt
OCTOBER
French Star
Log Cabin
Rob Peter & Pay Paul
Cherry Basket
Wedding Ring
NOVEMBER
Jacob's Ladder
Greek Cross
Sky Rocket
Double T
DECEMBER
Ocean Wave
Wild Goose Chase
Old Maid's Puzzle
Rambler

JANUARY 1929
Weathervane
Monkey Wrench
Spider Web
Irish Chain
FEBRUARY
Rising Sun
Princess Feather
Double Nine Patch
Eight-Pointed Star
MARCH
Goose in the Pond
Dove in the Window
Beautiful Star
Broken Circle
Beggar Block
APRIL
Cupid's Arrow Point
Noon Day Lily

Lafayette Orange Peel
Necktie
MAY
Duck and Ducklings
House on the Hill
Crossed Canoes
Turkey Tracks
JUNE
Ribbon Border Block
Posey
Bird's Nest
Crosses and Losses
Double Star
JULY
Jack in the Box
Aircraft
Springtime Blossoms
Sunbeam
AUGUST
Saw-Tooth
Cross and Crown
Hands All 'Round
Honey Bee
Flower Pot

SEPTEMBER
Susannah
Goose Tracks
Fish Block
Wedding Ring
OCTOBER
Swastika
Seth Thomas Rose
"V" Block
Little Beech Tree
NOVEMBER
Palm Leaf
Tulip Applique
Mill Wheel
Order No. 11
Old King Cole's Crown
DECEMBER
Strawberry Block
Old King Cole
Little Wooden Soldier
Road to Oklahoma
(The "Santa's Parade Quilt" series ran in December 1929).

JANUARY 1930
Churn Dash
Corn and Beans
Rose Cross
Milky Way
FEBRUARY
True Lovers Buggy Wheel
Indiana Puzzle
Blazing Star
Aster
MARCH
Sunflower
Grape Basket
Steps to the Altar
Kaleidoscope
Dutchman's Puzzle
APRIL
English Flower Garden
Single Wedding Ring
Pin Wheels
Cross and Crown
MAY
Missouri Puzzle
Merry Go-Round

Lone Star
Missouri Star
Sail Boat
JUNE
Virginia Star
Rail Fence
JULY
Mexican Star
Basket of Oranges
Rose Album
Clay's Choice
AUGUST
Maple Leaf
Sunbonnet Sue
Compass
Kaleidoscope
Rainbow Tile
SEPTEMBER
Goblet
Calico Puzzle
Broken Dishes
Swallows in the Window
OCTOBER
Secret Drawer
Spider Web
Marble Floor

Pinwheel (The "Memory Bouquet Quilt" series ran in October 1930.)
NOVEMBER
Grandmother's Favorite
Indian Emblem
Friendship
Puss in the Corner
Sage-Bud
(The "Memory Bouquet Quilt" series ran in November 1930).
DECEMBER
Turnabout "T"
Snow Crystals
Sweet Gum Leaf
Rose Dream

JANUARY 1931
Silver and Gold
Tennessee Star
Flower Pot
Greek Cross
Sheep Fold
FEBRUARY
Amethyst
Wheel of Mystery
Pontiac Star
Baby Bunting
MARCH
Seven Stars
Rebecca's Fan
French Bouquet
Casement Window
APRIL
Basket of Lilies
King's Crown

star quilts: year by year

June Butterfly
Fence Row
MAY
Indian Trail
English Ivy
Jackson Star
Dutch Tulip
Love Ring
JUNE
Ararat
Iris Leaf
Ozark Diamond
Kite Quilt
JULY
Cactus Flower
Arrowhead Star
Giddap
Sugar Loaf
AUGUST
Cross Roads
Bachelor's Puzzle
Morning Star
Pineapple Quilt
Dresden Plate
SEPTEMBER
Stepping Stones
Tennessee Star
Chips and
Whetstones
Boutonniere
OCTOBER
Prickly Pear
Castle Wall
Butterfly
Pickle Dish
Dutch Tile
NOVEMBER
Cottage Tulips
Formosa Tea Leaf
Bridge
Evening Star
DECEMBER
Poinsettia
Goldfish

Christmas Star
Crazy Daisy

JANUARY 1932
Friendship Knot
Circular Saw
Heart's Desire
Job's Tears
Necktie
(Horn of Plenty
Quilt series also ran
in January 1932).
FEBRUARY
Autograph Quilt
Hour-Glass
Spring Beauty
Grandmother's
Basket
(The "Horn of Plenty
Quilt" series also ran
in February 1932).
MARCH
Grandmother's
Favorite
Quilting Design
Shamrock
Magnolia Bud
APRIL
Nose-Gay
Diamond Field
Red Cross
Solomon's Puzzle
"4-H" Club
MAY
Russian Sunflower
Storm at Sea
Crow's Nest
Garden Maze
JUNE
Cowboy's Star
Ducklings
Lend and Borrow
Wheel of Fortune

JULY
Flying Bats
Log Cabin
Gretchen
Double Nine Patch
Kansas Star
AUGUST
Liberty Star
Golden Glow
Square Deal
Purple Cross
SEPTEMBER
Farmer's Wife
Interlocked Squares
Dove in the Window
Florida Star
OCTOBER
Interlocked Squares
Pineapple Cactus
Crazy Anne
Old Missouri
Clam Shells
(A diagram of the
"Happy Childhood
Quilt" ran in October
1932.
NOVEMBER
Puss in the Corner
Christmas Tree
Christmas Toy Quilt
Four Winds (The
"Happy Childhood
Quilt" also ran in
October 1932.
DECEMBER
Corner Posts
Snow Crystal
Pilot's Wheel
Christmas Tree
Star of Hope

JANUARY 1933
Star of Hope
Old Spanish Tile

Arkansas Star
Star-shaped
Quilting Design
Floral Pattern
Quilting Design
FEBRUARY
Sunflower Motif
Quilting Design
Petal and Leaf
Quilting Design
Medallion Quilting
Design
Pilot's Wheel
MARCH
Arkansas Star
Lone Star of
Paradise
Bouquet in a Fan
Nest and Fledgling
APRIL
St. Gregory's Cross
Guiding Star
Light and Shadow
Flowing Ribbon
Friendship Star
MAY
Broken Crown
Square Within
Square
Oklahoma Sunburst
Points and Petals
JUNE
Square and Points
Little Giant
Puss in the Corner
Double Arrow
JULY
Bridal Stairway
Air-Ship Propeller
Bridge Quilt
Indian Canoes
Flying Swallows
AUGUST
Double Pyramid

Economy
Triplet
Jack in the Pulpit
SEPTEMBER
Broken Stone
Cypress
Cheyenne
Glory Block
OCTOBER
Square and Half
Square
NOVEMBER
Poinsettia
Ozark Trail
Four Crown
Crow's Nest
DECEMBER
Circle Upon Circle
Arkansas
Christmas Tree
Morning Glory
Charm Quilt

JANUARY 1934
Star Center on
French Bouquet
Double Irish Chain
London Stairs
Franklin D.
Roosevelt
FEBRUARY
New Album
Valentine Quilt
Dogwood Blossom
Cat's Cradle
MARCH
Kansas Trouble
Water Glass
Eight Pointed Star
Broken Circle
Little Boy's
Breeches
APRIL
Pin-Wheel

Jinx Star
Oklahoma Sunburst
Texas Pointer
MAY
Snowball Quilt
Windmill Star
Flowering Nine-
Patch
Joseph's Coat
JUNE
Christmas Tree
Lover's Lane
Crystal Star
Wagon Wheels
Friendship Quilt
JULY
Triple Star
Gordian Knot
Red Cross
Airplane
AUGUST
Japanese Garden
Feather Edge Star
Saw Tooth
Sunflower Design
Pattern
SEPTEMBER
Dogwood Design
Pattern
Border and Block
Design Pattern
Lotus Leaf Design
Pattern
Whirling Pin Wheel
New Album
OCTOBER
Hazel Valley Cross
Roads
Jacob's Ladder
Arrow Star
Friendship Quilt
NOVEMBER
Quilting Motif
Design Pattern

Square Design
Pattern
Floral Motif Design
Pattern
Quilts and Gifts
Design Pattern
DECEMBER
Marble Quilt
Cluster of Lillies

JANUARY 1935
Arabic Lattice
Coffee Cups
Fan Quilt
FEBRUARY
Old-Fashioned
String Quilt
Arkansas Snowflake
Friday the 13th
Wedding Ring
MARCH
Missouri Daisy
Bridle Path
Farmer's Daughter
Arabic Lattice
APRIL
My Graduation
Class Ring
Goldfish
Ozark Trail
Tulip Quilt
MAY
Grandmother's
Basket
Churn Dash
Twinkle, Twinkle
Little Star
Indian Hatchet
Old Missouri
JUNE
String Quilt
Strawberry
Florida Star
Twinkle, Twinkle
Little Star
JULY
Jacob's Ladder
Sonnie's Play House

Shaded Trail
Grandma's Brooch
Flower Basket
AUGUST
Wind Mill
Diamond Circle
Railroad Crossing
Leaves and Flowers
Teapot
SEPTEMBER
Gold Bloom
Hands All Around
Apple Leaf
Four Leaf Clover
OCTOBER
Melon Patch
Arkansas Meadow
Rose
Scrap Bag
Pine Cone
Album
NOVEMBER
Squirrel in a Cage
Cog Wheels
Snail Trail
Compass and Chain
Broken Branch
DECEMBER
Basket of Flowers
Ozark Star
Shaded Trail
Kansas Dust Storm

JANUARY 1936
Missouri Wonder
Flower of Spring
Circle Saw
Arrow Head
FEBRUARY
Morning Star
White Lily
Seven Stars
Kansas Beauty
Young Man'
Invention
MARCH
Wood Lily or Indian
Head

Star Sapphire
Pointing Star
IXL or I Excel
APRIL
Butterfly
Dove at the Window
Quilter's Pride
Martha Washington
MAY
Dog Quilt
Patriotic Star
Ma Perkin's Flower
Garden
Cups and Saucers
Sickle
JUNE
Dove at the Window
Turkey Tracks
Jupiter Star
Lover's Link
JULY
Hidden Star
Airport
Marble Quilt

AUGUST
Anna's Pride
Star
SEPTEMBER
Whirligig Hexagon
Landon Sunflower
Chinese Puzzle
Rising Sun
OCTOBER
Ozark Cobblestone
Peggy Anne's
Special
Happy Hunting
Grounds
Mayflower
Dragonfly
NOVEMBER
Basket of Diamonds
Mountain Road
Solomon's Temple
Rolling Stone
DECEMBER
Circle and Square

Grandmother's Tulip
Modern Broken Dish

JANUARY 1937
The Kite
Arkansas Centennial
Flower Pot
Square Diamond
Whirling Star
FEBRUARY
Nosegays
Four-Pointed Star
Golden Circle Star
MARCH
Right Hand of
Fellowship
Waves of the Sea
Spool Quilt
Old-Fashioned
Goblet
Double "T"
APRIL
Quilt Without a
Name
Dolly Madison
Ozark Tile
Star of Bethlehem
MAY
Owl Quilt
Flower Garden Block
Depression
Diamond Cross
Winding Blade
Maple Leaf
JUNE
Album Quilt
Old Maid's Puzzle
Midget Necktie
JULY
Flying Kite
Double Square
Indian Star
Russian Sunflower
AUGUST
Ozark Sunflower
Hanging Basket
Basket of Diamonds
Broken Dish

SEPTEMBER
Verna Belle's
Favorite
Broken Window
Old-Fashioned Quilt
Bear's Paw
Arrowhead
Necktie
OCTOBER
Modern Broken Dish
Clay's Choice
Winged Square
Quilting Design for
Many Quilts
Lotus Quilting
Design
NOVEMBER
Modified Floral
Quilting Design
Circular Quilting
Design
Tulip Motif Quilting
Design
Conventional
Quilting Design
Favorite Quilting
Design
DECEMBER
Motif Quiltin Design
Household Quilting
Design

JANUARY 1938
Quilt of Variety
Ladies' Aid Album
Old-Fashioned
Wheel
FEBRUARY
Electric Fan
MARCH
Border Quilting
Design
Fair and Square
Texas Flower
APRIL
Twentieth Century
Star
Broken Square

Letha's Electric Fan
MAY
Jig Jog Puzzle
Bethlehem Star
Basket
Rebecca's Fan
North Star
Friendship Quilt
JUNE
Pin Wheel
Blockade
JULY
Chinese Block
Little Boy's
Breeches
Heart of the Home
AUGUST
Versatile Quilting
Design
Friendship Quilt
Maple Leaf
SEPTEMBER
Double Cross
Friendship Quilt
OCTOBER
Six-Pointed Star
Flying "X"
NOVEMBER
Contrary Husband
Floating Clouds
Right Hand of
Fellowship
White Square
DECEMBER
Wild Goose

JANUARY 1939
Sandhills Star
FEBRUARY
"T" Quilt
Small Wedding Ring
MARCH
Windmill
Wandering Flower
Pig Pen
APRIL
Farmer's Field
Sun Rays

star quilts: year by year

MAY
Swastika
Thrifty Wife
Crazy Tile
Chisholm Trail
JUNE
Lost Golsin'
Hexagon Beauty
Oak Grove Star
Pride of Ohio
JULY
"X" Quartette
Double "T"
Rolling Stone
AUGUST
Pine Burr
Corner Star
Broken Star
SEPTEMBER
Little Boy's Britches
Rosebud
Star and Box
Red Cross
OCTOBER
Our Country
Lost Paradise
Broken Path
NOVEMBER
Crown of Thorns
Flag In, Flag Out
Buckeye Beauty
DECEMBER
Rosalia Flower
Garden
Sylvia's Bow
Thrifty

JANUARY 1940
Air Plane
Bluebell
Ladies' Fancy
FEBRUARY
4-H
Six Point String

Little Cedar Tree
MARCH
Hicks Basket
Fan and Ring
APRIL
Silent Star
Cabin Windows
MAY
Mother's Favorite
Star
Comfort Quilt
Around the World
Flower Ring
JUNE
Mona's Choice
Long 9 Patch
Garden Walk
JULY
The "X"
Double "V"
Whirl Around
AUGUST
E-Z Quilt
Jig Saw Puzzle
Quilter's Fan
SEPTEMBER
Car Wheel
Winged Nine Patch
Spider Web
OCTOBER
Hexagon Star
Garden Patch
NOVEMBER
Southside Star
DECEMBER
Carrie Nation
Spool Quilt
Springtime in the
Ozarks
Four Patch Fox and
Goose

JANUARY 1941
Colorado Quilt

Red Cross
FEBRUARY
Mother's Choice
Cotton Boll
Anna's Choice
MARCH
Four Red Hearts
Arkansas Cross
Roads
Arrowhead
APRIL
Seven Sisters
Whirling Star
Mosaic
MAY
Missouri Sunflower
Fence Row
Wagon Wheels
JUNE
Fish Quilt
JULY
May Basket
Periwinkle
Quint Five
"H" Square
AUGUST
Starry Heavens
Friendship Chain
Flowers in a Basket
Contrary Wife
SEPTEMBER
Star Spangled
Banner
1941 Nine Patch
Quilt in Light and
Dark
OCTOBER
Four Buds
Radio Windmill
Four Leaf Clover
NOVEMBER
Buzz Saw
Star of Alamo
Winding Blade

Kitchen Woodbox
DECEMBER
Friendship Ring
Whirling Five Patch
Old Indian Trail
Mexican Star

JANUARY 1942
Sunlight and
Shadows
Ice Cream Cone
Arrowheads
Molly's Rose Garden
FEBRUARY
Tulips
Postage Stamp
Chain Quilt
MARCH
Four O' Clock
APRIL
Long Pointed Star
Victory Quilt
Victory Quilt in
Another Version
MAY
Salute to the Colors
Ola's Quilt
Rosebud
Depression Quilt
JUNE
Airplane
Danish Stars
Signal Lights
Shepherd's Crossing
JULY
London Stairs
Spider Web
Broken Sugar Bowl
AUGUST
Thorny Thicket
Envelope Motif
SEPTEMBER
Red and White
Crisscross

Drunkard's Trail
All-Over Pattern of
Octagons
OCTOBER
Full Moon
Red Cross
NOVEMBER
Ocean Wave
Modern Version of
String Quilt
Kansas Dugout
DECEMBER
Jerico Walls
Basket Quilt in
Triangles
Cornerstone
Pattern of Chinese
Origin

JANUARY 1943
Turtle on a Quilt
Red-White-Blue
Color Scheme
Carrie's Favorite
Applique
FEBRUARY
Quilting Design in
Points
Envelope
MARCH
Adaptations of the
Indian Trail
Builder's Block Quilt
APRIL
Salute to Loyalty
Octagons and
Squares
MAY
Evelyne's Whirling
Dust Storm
Army Star
JUNE
Broken Dish
Spider Web

JULY
Mountain Peak
Four-Corner Puzzle
Texas Trellis
AUGUST
Winding Blades
Reminiscent of the
Wedding Ring
SEPTEMBER
Ice Cream Cone
Whirling Pinwheel
Broken Wheel
OCTOBER
Fence Row
World Fair
NOVEMBER
Lone Star
DECEMBER
Formal Flower Bed
Patchwork Cushion
Top
Mowing Machine

JANUARY 1944
Striped Plain Quilt
FEBRUARY
Butterfly in Angles
Washington Stamp
MARCH
Whirling Blade
Jack in the Pulpit
Evening Star
APRIL
Friendship Name
Chain
MAY
Rosebud
President Roosevelt
New Four Pointer
JUNE
Sailboat Oklahoma
JULY
Blue Blades Flying

Outside the box.

AUGUST
Soldier Boy
Seven Stars
Solomon's Puzzle
SEPTEMBER
Roads to Berlin
Envelope Quilt
Victory Boat
OCTOBER
Goose Track
NOVEMBER
Hearts and
Diamonds in
Applique
This and That
DECEMBER
Irish Chain

JANUARY 1945
Gate or "H" Quilt
Oklahoma Star
FEBRUARY
Diamonds and
Arrow Points
MARCH
Morning Sun
Southern Star
APRIL
Scottish Cross
MAY
Friendship Quilt
Parallelogram Block
JUNE
Log Cabin
Grandmother's
Cross
JULY
Little Wedding Ring
Diversion Quilt
AUGUST
Four Diamonds
Arkansas Traveler
Field Flower
Applique
SEPTEMBER
Quilt Mosaic
Modern Envelope
OCTOBER

Baby Fan Applique
Circle in a Frame
NOVEMBER
Small Triangle
Sailboat in Blue and
White
Dove at the Window

FEBRUARY 1946
Fenced-In Star
Cup and Saucer
MARCH
Simplicity's Delight
APRIL
Double Irish Chain
Wee Fan
Basket of Bright
Flowers n May
Basket
JULY
Semi-Circle Saw
Meadow Rose
Steps to the Altar
AUGUST
White Cross
May Basket for
Applique
OCTOBER
Return of the
Swallows
NOVEMBER
Rose Dream
DECEMBER
Mother's Choice

JANUARY 1947
Red Cross
FEBRUARY
Springtime
Blossoms
MARCH
Ratchet Wheel
APRIL
Airplane Motif
Little Boy's Britches
Pieced Sunflower
JUNE
Road to Oklahoma

Mystery Snowball
Hen and Her Chicks
Tulip Quilt
JULY
Four-Leaf Clover
Wedding Ring
AUGUST
Friendship Quilt
Cottage Tulips
SEPTEMBER
May Basket in Floral
Tones
Century-Old Tulip
Pattern
OCTOBER
Frame with
Diamonds
Compass Quilt
Builder's Blocks
NOVEMBER
Carrie Nation
DECEMBER
Broken Star
Double "T"
Christmas Star

JANUARY 1948
Steps to the Altar
Crazy Tile
4-Part Strip Block
FEBRUARY
Circle Upon Circle
Stepping Stones
MARCH
Wagon Wheels
Boutonniere
APRIL
Spider Web
Liberty Star
Spring Beauty
JUNE
Spool Quilt
Royal Diamonds
JULY
Double Irish Chain
Sea Shell
AUGUST
Milkmaid's Star

Fans and a Ring
Thrifty Wife
SEPTEMBER
Pig Pen
Log Cabin
OCTOBER
Arkansas Star
Old Spanish Tile
NOVEMBER
Grandmother's Quilt
Whirling Diamonds
DECEMBER
Three-In-One
Star Chain
Granny's Choice

JANUARY 1949
Crown of Thorns
Betty's Delight
Tulip Pattern in High
Colors
FEBRUARY
Long Nine Patch
MARCH
Autograph Quilt
North Star
Lace Edge
APRIL
Flash of Diamonds
Terrapin
MAY
Magnolia Bud
Kansas Star
JUNE
Crazy Anne
Chips and
Whetstones
SEPTEMBER
Hollows and
Squares
Bright Jewel
OCTOBER
Gay Dutch Tile
Greek Cross
Ducklings for
Friendship
Arrowhead Star

NOVEMBER
Pussy in the Corner

JANUARY 1950
Broken Stone
FEBRUARY
Love in a Tangle
Bleeding Heart
Missouri Morning
Star
Queen Charlotte's
Crown
MARCH
Snowball
APRIL
Grandma's
Hopscotch
Triangles and
Squares
MAY
Jewel Quilt
Wishing Ring
JUNE
Oklahoma String
Scottie Quilt for
Boys
JULY
Whirligig
AUGUST
Little Girl's Star
Yellow Square
SEPTEMBER
Rainbow Quilt
OCTOBER
Parquetry for a Quilt
Block
NOVEMBER
Christmas Tree
Feather-Bone Block
DECEMBER
Spindles and
Stripes

JANUARY 1951
Little Wedding Ring
FEBRUARY
Picture Frames

MARCH
Box of Tulips
Remnant Ovals
Star in a Square
Four Vases
APRIL
Heirloom Jewel
MAY
Flower Garden
Mother's Choice
JUNE
Soldier Boy
JULY
4-Square Block with
Diamonds
Heart for Applique
SEPTEMBER
Panel of Roses
Whirling Windmill
OCTOBER
Block of Many
Triangles
Name is Hesper
DECEMBER
Spool Quilt
Brave Sunflower

JANUARY 1952
Winged Four-Patch
MARCH
Golden Wedding
Ring
Pickle Dish
APRIL
My Little Girl's Skirt
Broken Dish
MAY
Applique in Fruit
JUNE
Wagon Wheels
Carry Me Home
JULY
Star of Four Points
Rose for Elsa's
Pride
AUGUST
Design for
Patriotism

star quilts: year by year

My Mother's Apron
SEPTEMBER
Block of Many
Triangles
Triangles and
Squares
NOVEMBER
Wheel of Fortune
DECEMBER
Broken Circle

JANUARY 1953
Log Cabin
Swords and
Plowshares
FEBRUARY
Double Square
APRIL
Patty's Summer
Parasol
8-Point Snowflake
MAY
Multiple Square
Quilt
JUNE
Snowflake
Continuity
Signature
Friendship Quilt
Sea Shells on the
Beach
JULY
Basket-Weave
Friendship Block
Four Winds
AUGUST
Pin Wheel
SEPTEMBER
Sapphire Quilt
Block
OCTOBER
Double Irish Chain

NOVEMBER
Blazing Star
DECEMBER
Builder's Blocks

JANUARY 1954
Picket Fence
Star Garden
FEBRUARY
Signature Quilt
Dragon Fly
MARCH
Crystal Star
MAY
Rosebuds of Spring
JUNE
Dessert Plate
Circle Saw
JULY
Greek Cross
Thousand Stars
SEPTEMBER
Eight Points in a
Square
NOVEMBER
Windmill Blades

JANUARY 1955
Squares and
Triangles
Valentine Quilt
FEBRUARY
Wedding Ring
MARCH
My Country, For
Loyalty
APRIL
Journey to
California
Pointed Ovals
JUNE
Give This One a
Name

JULY
Fool's Square
Solomon's Temple
Old-Fashioned
Wagon Wheel
Cog Block
AUGUST
Garden of Flowers
Many Roads to the
White House
Petal Circle in a
Square
Irish Chain Hint
SEPTEMBER
Name on Each Line
Moon is New
Hobby Nook
Picture Frame
OCTOBER
Scrap Zigzag
NOVEMBER
End of the Road
Cross Patch
Double Anchor
DECEMBER
Old-Fashioned
Goblet
The Red, the White,
the Blue
Roman Stripe
Old English
Wedding Ring

JANUARY 1956
Nine Patch Star
Road to Oklahoma
Puss in the Corner
FEBRUARY
Rising Sun
True America
Bow Tie in Pink and
White

MARCH
Monkey Wrench
Diamond Cluster in
Frame
APRIL
Square and
Diamonds
Great Circle
Quilt for a 4-H Club
Room
MAY
Jupiter of Many
Points
JUNE
Road to Arkansas
Spearheads and
Quarter-Circles
Whirligig for Your
Child
JULY
Oklahoma Wonder
Hands All 'Round
AUGUST
Orange Peel
Caps for Witches
and Dunces
Star of the West
Rosette of Points
SEPTEMBER
Diamonds in the
Corners
Rising Sun
String Quilt in a Sea
Shell
OCTOBER
Pictures in the
Stairwell
Name on Each
Friendship Block
Texas or Lone Star
Design in
Geometrics

NOVEMBER
Little Wedding Ring
DECEMBER
Old-Fashioned Star
Quilt
Sunburst Quilt
Necktie

JANUARY 1957
Quilt Takes Patriotic
Hues
FEBRUARY
Jewels in a Frame
APRIL
Star of Diamond
Points
Oklahoma's
Semi-Centennial
MAY
Sail Boat
JULY
Soldier at the
Window
Broken Star
AUGUST
Oil Fields of
Oklahoma
SEPTEMBER
Windmills All
Around
OCTOBER
Oklahoma's Square
Dance
NOVEMBER
Road to Oklahoma

JANUARY 1958
Cross is Mother's
Choice
FEBRUARY
Old-Fashioned Pin
Wheel
Missouri Daisy

APRIL
Basket Weave
Friendship Quilt
MAY
Hicks Flower Basket
JUNE
Old Indian Trail
Ocean Wave of
Many Prints
AUGUST
Scrap Collector's
Quilt
Hour Glass in a
New Picture
SEPTEMBER
Seven Stars
Dogwood Blossom
Friendship Block in
Diamonds
NOVEMBER
Flying Colors

JANUARY 1959
Coverlet in Jewel
Tones
MARCH
Drunkard's Path
APRIL
Old-Fashioned
Indian Puzzle
Wedding Ring
JUNE
Spider Web Gone
Awry
JULY
6-Point Flower
Garden
Ferris Wheel
AUGUST
From a
Grandmother's
Collection

acknowledgements

Many thanks to the ladies who made our hexagon blocks and tested the patterns. This book wouldn't exist without them. They include Sharon McMillan (my big sister), Marquette Heights, Illinois; Peggy McFeeters, Morton, Illinois; Sue McNamara, Peoria, Illinois; and Debbie Pulley, Peoria, Illinois. My friends from Calico Cutups also helped on this project. They are; Florence Bessmer, Buckner, Missouri; Ruby Downing, Oak Grove, Missouri; Grace Spencer, Lexington, Missouri; Clara Diaz, Independence, Missouri; Rosemary Garten, Independence, Missouri; Donna English, Independence, Missouri; Arlene Johnson, Kansas City, Missouri; Alta Short, Independence, Missouri; Mary Ellen Bloomquist, Independence, Missouri; Donna Walz, Kansas City, Missouri and Corky and Peggy Hutinett of Raytown, Missouri.

I appreciate all the responses to our request for quilts to photograph for this book. Some people came from quite a distance and I'm most grateful to them for letting us enjoy their quilts and their stories.

Thanks also to Tammy Ljungblad for her lovely photographs, to Jeff Dodge for his elegant book design, and to Doug Worgul for his patient editing. -*Edie McGinnis*

From left: Ozark Star block. Made by Peggy McFeeters of Morton, Illinois; Pointing Star block. Made by Debbie Pulley of Peoria, Illinois; Dutch Tile, made by Florence Bessmer, Buckner, Missouri.

about the author

Edie McGinnis has been a quilter and quilting teacher for about 25 years. She was a member of Boonslick Trail Quilting Guild in Columbia, Missouri, and is presently a member of the American Quilter's Society and the Calico Cut-ups Quilting Club of Independence, Missouri. This is Edie's second book about the Kansas City Star Quilt patterns.